HEAL & AWAKEN THE GODDESS WITHIN

Living a Life of Meaning and Purpose

GENEVIEVE TAEGER

Copyright © 2022 by Genevieve Taeger

All rights reserved. No part of this publication may be reproduced in any form or by any means, electronic or mechanical, including photocopying, recording, or any information browsing, storage, or retrieval system, other than for "fair use" as brief quotations embodied in articles and reviews, without permission in writing from the Author.

Published by Live A Transformative Life,
connect@liveatransformativelife.com

1st Edition - December 2022

Cover Art by Ahmat Wirogati. To purchase Original Paintings or Prints of Heal & Awaken the Goddess Within Oracle Cards, contact Genevieve Taeger at connect@liveatransformativelife.com.

The Reader is solely responsible for creating and implementing the Reader's own physical, mental and emotional well-being. The author is neither liable nor responsible for any actions or inaction taken and for any direct or indirect result of the information provided in this book. The Reader understands the guidance in this book is not therapy and does not substitute for treatment if needed. The information given in this book should not be treated as a substitute for professional medical advice; always consult a medical practitioner.

DEDICATION

For the Goddesses and Benevolent Realm—You asked, and I delivered. I'm eternally grateful for your neverending Love, Support and Sacred Guidance.

To my Beloved Mother and Father, who spent years dedicating their lives to the Awakening of Humanity.

And to my Husband, Stephen Shaw, who consistently supports me in furthering this Awakening. I love you.

CONTENTS

INTRODUCTION

Welcome to Your Sacred Journey 1

CHAPTER 1

Feeling Alone 15

Initiation: Making Room for the Inner Goddess.................................20

Mother Mary, Jesus, and Serapis Bey...20

CHAPTER 2

Releasing Anxiety...27

Exercise: Triggers..29

Exercise: Returning to Wholeness...30

Initiation: Returning to Wholeness 32

Goddess Sophia and Goddess Diana 32

CHAPTER 3

Clearing Ancestral Trauma..39

Exercise: Clearing Ancestral Trauma 41

Initiation: Clearing Ancestral Trauma..43

Goddess Isis and the Lyran Realm 43

CHAPTER 4

Honouring the Sacred Body 49

Exercise: Inviting Healthy Foods into the Body..................................51

Exercise: Honouring Your Body 54

Initiation: Honouring Your Body...55

The Goddess Realm 55

i

CHAPTER 5

Healing the Illusion of Fear 61

Exercise: Releasing Resistance 62

Initiation & Activation: Divine Essence of Love, Wisdom, and Power 65

Goddess Quan Yin and Goddess Emmanuella 65

CHAPTER 6

Shifting Your Focus on the Divine Mind 73

Exercise: Awaken to Your Thoughts 75

Exercise: Opening Awareness to The Divine Mind 76

Initiation: Opening Awareness to The Divine Mind 78

Lord Lanto 78

CHAPTER 7

Removing Stressors from Your Life 83

Exercise: Letting go of Stressors 85

Initiation & Activation: Awakening to Your Divine Passions 87

Goddess Quan Yin and Archangel Raphael 87

CHAPTER 8

Embracing Your Divine Passions 93

Exercise: Becoming Aware of Your Passions 96

Initiation & Activation: Embodying Your Divine Passions 98

Beloved Mary Magdalene 98

CHAPTER 9

Awakening to Your Divine Strengths 105

Exercise: Becoming Aware of Your Strengths 106

Exercise: Becoming Aware of Your Strengths From Past Lives 106

Initiation & Activation: Twining Your Rope of Divine Passions with Your Divine Strengths 109

Mary Magdalene and Goddess Peddamma 109

CHAPTER 10

Mapping Out Your Divine Purpose 117

Exercise: Heartstorming 118

Exercise: Mapping Out Your Divine Purpose.. 121

Initiation: Celebration of Awakening to Your Divine Purpose 123

Goddesses Athena and Mary Magdalene 123

CHAPTER 11

Embracing Your Divine Power 131

Exercise: Aligning with Your Divine Purpose 133

Initiation & Activation: Aligning with the Power of Divine Will............. 137

The Divine and your Holy Spirit 137

CHAPTER 12

Calling Forth the Action Taker Within You 143

Exercise: Discovering the Actions You Can Take 145

Initiation: Soaring with the Divine Eagle Within You 149

Eagle Spirit 149

CHAPTER 13

Aligning with Positively Driven People.. 155

Exercise: Becoming Aware of Whom You are Aligned With 158

Exercise: Inviting New Loved Ones Into Your Life 159

Initiation: Reuniting with Your Divine Soul Family.............................. 161

Goddess Daphne and Goddess Sophia 161

CHAPTER 14

Healing from Corporate Mentality Mindset 169

Exercise: Becoming Aware of Corporate Mentality Mindset 172

Initiation: Taking Back Your Freedom 174

Elephant Spirit and Goddess Athena 174

CHAPTER 15

Embracing Money 181

Exercise: Respecting the Tides of Your Sacred Moon 182

Exercise: How You See Your Reflection 184

Exercise: Embracing Money 186

Initiation: Honouring the Sacred Moon Within You 188

Mother Moon Spirit 188

CHAPTER 16

Honouring Your Magnificence 195

Exercise: Becoming Aware of How Small You are Playing 197

Exercise: Creating Your Reality 198

Initiation & Activation: Honouring Your Magnificence 200

Goddess Athena 200

CHAPTER 17

Embracing Your Inner Saviour 205

Exercise: Inviting Trust Back Into Your Life 207

Initiation & Activation: Embracing Your Inner Saviour 209

Quan Yin and Archangel Raphael 209

CHAPTER 18

Going Deep 215

Exercise: Going Deep 217

Initiation: Going Deep 220

Goddess Hecate 220

CHAPTER 19

Aligning with Your Divine Purpose 227

Exercise: Vision Statement 228

Exercise: Mission Statement 230

Initiation & Activation: Holy of Holies 232

Lord Lanto and Mary Magdalene 232

CHAPTER 20

Being Grounded 237

Exercise: Groundedness Awareness 238

Exercise: Grounding 239

Initiation: Connecting with Great Gaia Spirit 242

Great Gaia Spirit 242

CHAPTER 21

Being Present 247

Exercise: Breath Awareness 249

Exercise: Breath Awareness During Daily Activities 250

Initiation: Becoming One with Your Inner Divine Presence ... 252

Buddha 252

CHAPTER 22

Coming Home 259

Exercise: Reflections on What I Need 268

Sacred Blessing: Coming Home 270

Beloved Mary Magdalene 270

About the Author 275

ACKNOWLEDGEMENT

This work is a culmination of all I have learned and experienced during the past half-century. Many beautiful Souls have helped me behind the scenes to be the person I am today.

Sophie Bashford, your dedication to your work and your steadfast commitment to being the Goddess's voice has helped me develop the courage to bring my gifts into the world. Thank you for being my mentor and pillar of hope for over a decade now.

William Lee Rand, enough cannot be said about how you and Reiki changed my life. When I found your Reiki Manual at Peace Place in Sedona, I felt I had finally found the teaching Manual I had been looking for. Your love and devotion to your work helped me carry it forward and help heal and awaken so many beautiful Souls.

Carolyn Musial, I will never forget that first day of class we had together. We felt like Sisters. I am forever grateful for your guidance and sweet support on my path with Reiki.

Laurelle Gaia, thank you for visiting me a few times during my sleep with your loving Holy Spirit as you encouraged me and guided me to play BIG. I listened to your Call.

Kim Steffler, thank you for being there for me and honouring me for over 30 years. You have been my rock and dear friend, and I am eternally grateful for our friendship. Thank you for blessing me with your vulnerability, joys and struggles and for sharing your Sacred Heart.

Alyssia Generali, our connection is beyond words. We are a part of each other—something that cannot be explained. Thank you for seeing my Holy Spirit and giving me the honour to see yours.

Gabriella Biro, you see me. Our connection is sacred, and our bond cannot be explained. I am so grateful you reminded me of who I am. Thank you for shining your beautiful light and for being my eternal Sister.

Atefeh Moghaddamzadeh, thank you for embracing my imperfect human side over the years and helping me to grow and become a better human being.

Malgorzata Lawska, my Spirit Sister, I am privileged that we finally found each other. You are the sister I always knew I had. Thank you for being so adept with your intuitive skills and providing loving guidance when I need it most. Thank you, too, for reuniting me back with my Spirit Brother.

Ahmat Wirogati, my Spirit Brother, words cannot describe the sacred connection we have. You see what I see. Thank you for respecting the Spirit Painter within you. You are my blood and always will be, as I promised you when we were brothers.

Kit Woods, your courage to be a leader in bringing out the Divine Teachings excited me and gave me hope and enthusiasm to share my Gifts in this world. Thank you for so many beautiful moments together and for having been my teacher and healer when I was first starting. I cannot thank you enough.

Charlene Bateman, your loyalty and support has been unwavering. Your contribution to this world has helped make this book happen. I do not say this lightly. Thank you for blessing me with your love.

Melissa Tomé, thank you for saying, "So, when are you going to do that thing you said you would be doing?" As soon as I heard those words from your lips, I smiled because I knew the Goddesses were talking to me. Thank you for listening and making this book happen sooner than later. I am blessed to have you a part of my life.

Peter Dennis, your kindness and encouragement touched me to the core. I am forever grateful to you for helping me to have the courage to channel again. Thank you, my friend.

Crystal Andrus Morissette, your bold and powerful Goddess energy struck me the first time I met you more than a decade ago at your retreat. Thank you for encouraging a plethora of women (including myself) to become a torch for the healing and uplifting of humanity.

Casey Paul, you have been a ray of incredible sunshine over the past year. You are such a powerful gift to this world. Thank you for cheering me on with the writing of this book.

Stuart Ross, thank you for awakening me to my treasure house of possibilities so I can be the best version of myself and offer these Gifts to the world.

Jason Kubassek and Steph Morris, thank you for believing in me and helping me to come out even more into the world. Your love has touched me deeply. Steph, thank you for helping me to honour the Goddess within.

Markus Kaltennegger, you are the best business accountability partner I could have. Thank you for your unending encouragement and challenging discussions. I'm forever grateful for our friendship.

To all the clients and students who have honoured me with receiving my channeled teachings and healings, it is you who have inspired me to create this book. Thank you for your never-ending commitment and support. I am humbled.

To all my friends, too many to name, thank you for touching my heart along the way and helping me to become who I am today.

Gerit Taeger, my Sacred Earth Mother, thank you for blessing me with your love, nurturing, and support my whole life.

To my late father, Bernd Taeger, thank you for opening me up to my Holy Spirit.

Clyde Taeger, my beautiful brother, thank you for your unceasing love and for making me laugh over the years. I needed that.

To my late brother, Derek Taeger, thank you for teaching me kindness and seeing the beautiful Divine Spirit in every human being.

And, finally, to my husband, Stephen Shaw, thank you for your Sacred Love, support, and encouragement. I wouldn't have wanted to do this without you. Your dedication to our union is beyond words. I love you.

INTRODUCTION

WELCOME TO YOUR SACRED JOURNEY

"You Get to Witness Yourself Uniting with Your Holy Spirit and Your Passionate Heart's Desires" - Mary Magdalene

Welcome, my friends. Welcome to this Sacred Journey you are about to embark upon. This is a journey of joyous revelation. It is here where you get to experience the shedding of the old and the bringing forth of the new. At the end of this book, you get to witness yourself uniting with the effervescence of your Holy Spirit and your Passionate Heart's desires. You will move forward with a Luminescent Body in union with the Divine. You will be empowered to liberate yourself to live a life of meaning and Purpose. You will have learned how to Awaken the Goddess Within. This applies to you no matter what gender you are or identify as.

For centuries, most of us have mastered utilizing the powerful qualities of our Inner Sacred Masculine Energy; however, most of us have suppressed our Inner Sacred Feminine qualities to keep us feeling safe due to trauma and societal conditioning. Every human being carries the Sacred Feminine and Sacred Masculine archetypal energy within themselves. We are meant to use *all* these beautiful qualities we were gifted with. Suppression of the Inner Sacred Feminine (Goddess Within) has resulted in most people losing touch with their intuition, not being able to birth their creations, and preventing themselves from fully discovering and expressing their Holy Spirit's desires. We have been so focused on the unique qualities of the Sacred Masculine that we have become out of balance and have lost touch with our true Purpose in life.

This book is created for every person who feels they haven't fully honoured the Sacred Feminine qualities within. If you think you lost a deeper connection with your intuitive side or could develop it more and haven't allowed yourself to connect with and be a full expression of your Holy Spirit's Purpose, this book is designed for you. It does not matter what gender you are or identify yourself as; if you do not feel completely in balance with the Divine Feminine and Masculine energy, this is for you.

You have come here to this book because you are ready to shed what no longer serves you. You are tired of being frustrated with not living your Purpose fully. You know there is something more significant for you, and although scary, you want to honour this Greater Calling but don't know how.

You have been feeling a nudging for quite some time now, and it feels painful knowing you are meant to do more and experience more joy and fulfillment in your life, yet it is not happening as it should be.

I know exactly how you may feel, as I was once there myself. It can feel lonely and frustrating because you know you have a greater Purpose. You can feel it, yet you may not know how to discover it if it hasn't been found yet. Or, you wonder what steps to take if you have uncovered your Purpose already. Due to all your responsibilities, you may think it is impossible to experience life the way you know you deserve to.

The Goddesses and Benevolent Realm are happy to tell you that a joyous and Purposeful life *is* possible. In fact, you came here to live this magnificent possibility.

INTRODUCTION

You don't have to live a life filled with struggle and compromises. You will soon learn that these thoughts are lies we have been telling ourselves.

You are meant to live a life that makes you pinch yourself as you wonder why you are here experiencing such elation. Hearing this may sound unreal, but I am here to help you unlearn all the false teachings we have been shown so that you may live a glorious life filled with Purpose and meaning.

I lived a life for 30 years in the Corporate world and moved myself up into a prominent position, taking on the role of a Director without having been honoured with the Official Title. I was overseeing the Health and Safety of a staff of 1,000 people in three manufacturing facilities in the automotive sector. I was "proudly" responsible for ensuring tools, equipment, and machinery were designed, built, and running safely. I had to ensure that Management, Supervisors, and Employees were trained accordingly and that all Policies and Procedures were developed according to the legal requirements. I was responsible for making sure these requirements were adhered to. This was a massive undertaking. It was a high-stress leadership role that required hours of my time and dedicated commitment never to give up while experiencing severe stress.

For years, I kept hoping things would get easier once everything was in place. Throughout most of these years of hoping, I felt the nudging from my Soul that I was meant to do, be, and experience more. I could feel my Soul telling me that there were more extraordinary things for me. I felt trapped in this situation and didn't know how to get out. I had bills to pay. A part of me loved the job, which confused me even more. "Why would I want to leave when this job means so much to me?" I asked myself. I kept feeling my instinct telling me, "You are meant to do and be so much more. You are meant to shine your light and help the world in a way you cannot even fathom." I heard the voice inside of me, but I couldn't entirely accept this was true. "It's impossible," I thought. "Why me? What makes me so unique?"

Does this sound familiar? Do you feel a nudging inside of you, yet you doubt that this could even remotely be true because the Calling feels so magnanimous? For some, this Calling isn't referring to having a different career. Some of you may feel a strong nudge to take part in life in a completely different way—perhaps through volunteering or philanthropy, or maybe by simply being a different kind of person in everything you do by expressing a special Gift of yours that you know will help humanity. I understand because I've been there myself.

The nudging we experience from within is because our Holy Spirit wants us to shine its Greatness in this world. "You didn't come to Earth to play small. You came here to illuminate your Magnificence," says the Goddess Realm.

We think it would be easier to keep the status quo, but we lie to ourselves when we say this. We default into numbing ourselves to keep feeling safe. This is how we have operated since we were young. It isn't our fault. This is how society has taught us to behave.

So, here we are, at the precipice of a New Age. "The time is nigh, Beloved Beings—The time is Nigh," says the Goddess Realm.

Over twenty years ago, when I was in my thirties, I started connecting with Ascended Masters and Angels. I was being guided regularly that, soon, these Benevolent Beings became my best friends. They loved me unconditionally and were always trying to direct me toward a better way of life. Yet, they often challenged me to take my Gifts and help humanity. The truth is, I was too scared to follow through on this Sacred Guidance until I had a breakdown when I turned 50. Little did I know that this was how my Soul and Holy Spirit were telling me, "Enough!" because I wasn't listening. I kept thinking that "one day," when I have time and fewer responsibilities, I will do what I want to do in life. I was secretly lying to myself and wasn't aware of my behaviour toward myself.

INTRODUCTION

After my breakdown, everything changed—I quit my job, sold my house, and vowed to have the courage to listen to my Heart and follow my Holy Spirit's Sacred Calling to live my Purpose. Once I made this vow, a world of possibilities opened up for me. A stream of Goddesses came through, instructing me to "write this book now because the world needs it."

You are here reading this book because I made a vow to heed and follow through with my Holy Spirit's Calling. The Goddesses asked me to write this book for you so that you can Heal & Awaken The Goddess Within, discover your Purpose and learn how you can take massive action steps toward living your Calling much sooner than later. You are meant to experience your Greatness *Now*.

I channeled this book from the Wisdom of the Goddesses, Benevolent Beings, and my Holy Spirit. I emphasize Goddesses because most of the Benevolent Beings who came to provide these teachings are Goddesses.

I use the word "Benevolent" for these Beings because they work hand in hand with the Divine. As you know, the Divine has many names—God, Allah, YHWH, Almighty, Universe, I AM THAT I AM, Elohim, Jehovah, Alpha and the Omega, the Light, Lord of Lords, Bhagavan, and Waheguru, to name a few. Please know that when I refer to the Divine, I am referring to the nameless One—the Source of all that is.

Goddesses and Benevolent Beings are here to serve you. Their sole purpose is to aid you in moving away from struggles so you can experience more ease and, ultimately, Enlightenment. When you experience Enlightenment, you are One with your Holy Spirit and the Divine; during this moment, you receive the Greatest Guidance possible because it comes from the Holy of Holies. They have shown me the steps you can take to experience this Great Bliss.

The Goddesses and Benevolent Beings have provided me with the teachings that serve your Higher Purpose. They say, "It is time, once and for all, to heal what is holding you back from experiencing what you came here to experience. You are meant for so much more than you have allowed yourself."

♦

How to Embark on Your Journey in this Book

The teachings have been laid out in the most beneficial order for you. It is important that you start from the beginning and go through the exercises in the order the chapters were given. Each chapter builds on the previous chapter, both in teachings and healings, at an energetic level. In other words, each chapter prepares you to receive the necessary healing and guidance for the next chapter.

This book takes you through incremental steps to:

- heal and transmute conscious and unconscious fears and anxiety (we have all carried unconscious traits of fears and anxiety, which I will explain later) that are holding you back from moving forward so you can finally get unstuck;
- awaken to your Holy Spirit and the Divine and discover your Sacred Purpose;
- empower you with action steps that you will *want* to take because you will have learned how to receive and welcome Guidance from the Divine Mind;
- create new neural pathways to align you with living your Purpose so that you don't revert to applying old patterned ways of doing things; and
- learn how to develop a continual connection with your Holy Spirit, Goddesses, Benevolent Beings, and the Divine so you can manifest your Greatness in the here and now.

INTRODUCTION

The Goddesses have taught me that we have been blocked and held frozen due to situations out of our control. Our past has impacted us from this life, past lives, and our ancestral lives. The good news is that they have taught me how to clear what has kept us frozen. With each chapter comes a Sacred Teaching. After each teaching, you are asked to do one to three exercises in your journal, depending on which chapter it is. The purpose of these exercises is to bring the unconscious to the surface. To heal, we must become the Observer of what needs healing.

After completing the exercise(s), you will read through an Initiation or an Initiation and Activation given to you from a particular Goddess or Benevolent Being. In some cases, more than one Goddess or Benevolent Being is giving the Initiation and Activation. With these Initiations and Activations come powerful healing. The Goddesses and Benevolent Realm are assisting with and providing this healing. Some of you may experience these beautiful, Sacred Benevolent Beings providing you with this healing. If you do not *feel* it, then please *know* that healing is definitely occurring. Some people are just more energetically sensitive, such as empaths. There was a time when I felt nothing. I couldn't sense, see, or intuit energy. It took years for me to be able to heighten all of my intuitive senses.

When you read through these Initiations and Activations, I recommend you utilize one of the following methods to experience the healing:

* Make a recording by reading out loud the Initiation and Activation. Allow pauses throughout to give yourself time to experience the healing. Make the recording approximately 15 minutes long so that you have ample time to experience the healing and glory of connecting with the teachings and with the Goddesses and Benevolent Beings.

* Read through a few sentences, then close your eyes and experience that part of the Initiation and Activation for a minute

or more. Open your eyes and read through the following few sentences, and experience the next part of the healing. Keep going in this manner until you have reached the end.

An Initiation will release what no longer serves you and empower you with what is best for you. Your energy body and physical body will vibrate at a higher frequency after the Initiation. An Activation will activate your Mind, Body, and Soul into a Sacred Teaching so you can walk with this new Knowledge as part of your everyday life. This means that the Energetic Quality of that teaching is activated within you, so you resonate energetically with the Guidance.

The exercise(s) you had just completed in the chapter assist with ensuring your Initiations and Activations are successful. To prepare for the meditation, allow yourself to relax and trust in the process. Know that what you are doing is perfect because your Soul and Holy Spirit Guide you through the process via your instinct. Sometimes, when I have taught Reiki, people have often asked me how they know that Reiki is working. The same answer applies here. A good way of realizing you received healing is noticing the changes within yourself over time. Keep a journal of circumstances, feelings, and behaviours you are experiencing so you can look back and see the shifts that have occurred. Also, notice what other people are saying about you. These help you to see the evidence that you received the healing.

At the end of each Initiation and Activation, I recommend you spend time grounding yourself to integrate the energy entirely. Taking walks in nature is a very effective way to feel grounded.

Your energy body will rise in frequency with each successive chapter. At the end of this book, your energy body will become lighter. You will feel a lightness of being. You may also experience Gravity differently as your body may feel lighter when moving it.

I cannot stress the importance of going through each chapter in the order given and ensuring you do each exercise as the Goddesses

INTRODUCTION

know precisely what you need to do to propel yourself forward to live a life of joy, meaning, and abundance.

◆

How to Use this Book in the Future

How to Use as a Reference After Completing Your Journey

In the future, you can consider this book a reference book for you to come back to again and again. Once you have completed this book, you can refer to a specific chapter to obtain the assistance you need to get past a hurdle. For example, you may have a challenge arise that may trigger a particular behaviour that is holding you back from moving forward. You can then go to the chapter in the book that will help you overcome this challenge.

You may wonder why you need to return to this book after completing it. The answer lies in understanding the Power of the Divine. The Divine is ever expansive, and, as a result, so are you. The more inner work you do on yourself, the greater the capacity to experience even more of your Holy Spirit and its Guidance. The more Guidance you receive from your Holy Spirit, the more you grow. Occasionally, you may notice your Holy Spirit showing you even more possibilities for growth than you would have imagined. This may trigger you to play small, stay at your new status quo, or even feel scared. When you notice these things occurring, you can gently and lovingly remind yourself to return to this book and turn to the chapter of your choice that would benefit you the most.

You may also return to this book to develop stronger connections with the Goddesses and Benevolent Beings that were here for you during your spectacular journey. You can always pick a Benevolent Being you would like to connect with, or you can even have fun, flip through the pages, and let your hand stop on one of them and discover which one is in that chapter you can connect with. The more you connect with them, the easier it becomes.

◆

Details on the Goddesses and Benevolent Beings

Qualities and Purpose

Twenty-two Goddesses and Benevolent Beings came through to provide teaching and healing. I have been guided not to tell you the history of these Goddesses and Benevolent Beings because they don't want you to focus on mythical stories from the past. They say that many of these stories are incorrect. People have often focused on the myth behind them rather than on the true purpose they serve for you now.

These Benevolent Beings are here to serve you and assist you on your path toward experiencing the best possible life you can live. Each Goddess and Benevolent Being focuses on a specialty they help people with. You can view them as ideal archetypes. When you have a challenging time with a particular type of emotion or topic, you can turn to the Goddess or Benevolent Being who specializes in this field. You can liken these Beings to specific frequencies. They hold the key to perfection in that particular topic.

The more you connect with them, the more you learn about them and discover their unique, beautiful qualities.

These Sacred Beings tend to focus on specific types of instructions, hence why each chapter has different Goddesses and Benevolent Beings coming through. Some have shown up multiple times in various parts of the book to assist with your healing. You can consider them as archetypes of particular topics. I will provide you with a summary of their specialties below in the order they arrived in the book:

INTRODUCTION

- Mother Mary helps with taking your sorrows away. She is the Eternal Mother here to support you whenever you need nurturing love and support.
- Jesus reunites you with the Holy Spirit and showers you with Divine Love.
- Serapis Bey recalibrates you with a connection to your Divine DNA and the Sacred Feminine energy within.
- Goddess Sophia assists you with your creations. She helps you to have your voice again and be free to express who you are. She unites you back with your Soul Family.
- Goddess Diana takes your troubles away that are stopping you from experiencing your wholeness. She utilizes the energy of the full moon to assist with this transmutation of what no longer serves you.
- Goddess Isis helps you become fully balanced with your masculine and feminine energies. She is a powerhouse. When you connect with her, you can experience the great masculine and feminine strengths rising within you.
- The Ascended Lyran Realm consists of Ascended Masters from the Lyran Constellation, and they are here to transmute all unconscious ancestral trauma in your cellular.
- The Goddess Realm is a realm of Goddesses assisting you in awakening all the Inner Sacred Feminine qualities of self-expression, sexuality, and creativity, to name a few.
- Quan Yin is the Goddess of mercy and compassion. She provides direction and comfort whenever you need to feel heard and understood. She helps you to surrender to yourself and turn inwards toward your Inner Saviour for strength, wisdom, and guidance.

- ❖ Goddess Emmanuella brings back your connection to the Essence of the Divine (pure qualities of Love, Wisdom, and Power) so that you may carry the spark of truth and awareness within you at all times.

- ❖ Lord Lanto aligns you with the Gateway to the Divine Mind, where you can access Divine Wisdom. He teaches you the principle of aligning with Inner Knowing so you can manifest your Sacred Desires Now.

- ❖ Archangel Raphael is the healing Archangel who helps you with anything that needs healing. This applies to you physically, mentally, emotionally, and spiritually.

- ❖ Mary Magdalene activates your Passionate Heart and opens the Gateway to your Divine Passions, your Holy Spirit, and the Holy of Holies. She is here to help steer you toward living your Purpose in alignment with your Divine Passions.

- ❖ Goddess Peddamma clears your Mind, Body, and Aura of demons (self-limiting beliefs) holding you back from living your life with Purpose and experiencing a joyous life.

- ❖ Goddess Athena is a Goddess Warrior assisting you to awaken the strength and courage within you to fight for your right to live your Divine Purpose. She awakens the Sacred Feminine quality of powerful self-expression. She helps you cast away all doubt and empowers you to restore your freedom. She aligns you with your Inner Magnificence.

- ❖ Eagle Spirit initiates you into the reunion with your Divine Eagle Spirit. He teaches you *how* to trust yourself so you can soar to great heights.

- ❖ Goddess Daphne is one with nature and helps you to connect to your inner core. She helps you to see your natural self. She shares Sacred Nature Teachings that you can apply to help steer you on your path.

INTRODUCTION

- ❖ Elephant Spirit brings back all aspects of yourself into this world. She empowers you to return to wholeness so you can create miracles and live the best version of yourself. She helps you to respect and honour yourself.

- ❖ Mother Moon Spirit empowers you to reflect your beauty in the world. She helps you to resonate with your Divine Worth. She teaches you the power of manifestation and abundance by feeling your brilliance and the beautiful impact you make in other people's lives. She helps you to learn the sacred teachings of money.

- ❖ Goddess Hecate assists with clearing conscious and unconscious trauma from this life, past lives, and ancestral lives. She helps you to liberate yourself to experience your greatest possible freedom and make powerful positive choices in your life.

- ❖ Great Gaia Spirit helps to ground you. She teaches you how awareness can help connect you to her energy and experience her Mightiness. You can also receive unrevealed teachings from the "Great Unknown," as she describes herself.

- ❖ Buddha helps you to experience the sacredness of your breath. He teaches you how to live in the Now through the practice of the awareness of your breath. Buddha teaches you how to experience your Inner Divine Presence.

One recommendation I have for you during your discovery time getting to know these precious Goddesses and Benevolent Beings is to be kind to yourself, have patience, and enjoy the journey. It can take time for people's sixth senses to open up. It certainly took me quite some time to open my clairsentience (clear feeling), claircognizance (clear knowing), clairvoyance (clear seeing), clairaudience (clear hearing), clairalience (clear smelling), and clairgustance (clear tasting). As you continue practicing awareness of the Divine, your meridian channels will open up more to receive energy. The more you receive energy, the more your meridian channels open up. The more your channels open up, the more aware you are of receiving guidance through your clairsenses.

Now is your time to enjoy the journey of this powerful transformation you are about to experience. Put your seatbelt on and enjoy the ride!

CHAPTER 1

FEELING ALONE

"You are not alone, Divine Ones. You just miss uniting with your Inner Goddess" - Mother Mary

When I look at so many of you, my heart aches because I know what you are feeling. You feel alone. You feel like no one truly sees you and feels you. No one truly gets what you deeply yearn for. Yet, you can't quite understand why you think this way. Often, you may have felt like you have very few people in your life who honestly know you. You may even feel alone amongst your partners or best friends, no matter how much you love them.

Guilt can set in because you tell yourself that you shouldn't feel this way with your closest connections. Yet you do.

Why?

Deep down inside, your Soul remembers home, and your Holy Spirit is nudging your Soul to let go of fear and express your Holy Spirit's desires while you are here on Earth.

Before I go any further, let me explain the concepts of Spirit and Soul.

Your Spirit is that part of you who was birthed from the Divine. Your Spirit is the purest part of you, having direct access to the Kingdom of Heaven. Your Spirit is the purest expression of the Divine. Your Spirit is always connected to Source as though it is standing under a waterfall of the Divine.

Your Soul is the instrument of the Holy Spirit. Your Soul was birthed to be an expression of your Holy Spirit. When your Soul is tapped into the waterfall of the Holy Spirit, it can access the greatness of the Divine and go forth and be the full expression of happiness, joy, abundance, and creativity in this world.

Your body is where your Soul can reside and animate the expression of the Divine. It is here, in your body, that you came to be, for a lifetime, to witness and experience the manifestations of your Holy Spirit's greatest desires.

We all have Sacred Feminine and Sacred Masculine qualities within ourselves, no matter what gender we identify with. The Goddess within you is the Sacred Feminine part of you, which is highly intuitive and desires to create and be a full expression of your Holy Spirit's greatest desires.

The Sacred Masculine part of you is the powerful action-taker. This is the part of you who goes forth and takes action on your desires.

For centuries now, we have suppressed the Goddess within. We have placed much more emphasis on the Sacred Masculine and, more often than not, have left the Sacred Feminine behind.

Now is the time to Heal and Awaken the Goddess Within, so we can open to our natural intuition and discover how to tap into our Spirit's desires, create immaculate manifestations and live a life of joy, abundance, and freedom.

FEELING ALONE

◆

"So why do I feel so incredibly alone?" you ask.

You are an awakened human being, even though you may not feel that at times. You have a claircognizance, a knowing, deep down inside you, that there is something greater within you. You sense there is something greater within you that needs to be expressed. This is your Divine Inner Goddess nudging you consistently, and it can make you feel alone because you see others who appear to be just fine living their day-to-day lives.

This nudging is asking you to feel A-L-I-V-E every single day. You feel this calling, yet you can't see people near you urgently wanting this. This makes you feel so alone because you wish to share these feelings, yet you know most people won't understand.

I am here to share with you right here and right now that I completely and fully understand.

Take a moment to breathe that in.

I understand.

You are not alone.

I understand.

◆

Making Room for the Inner Goddess Teaching

Preparation for Initiation

Everything in this world is made up of energy. There are various amplitudes of wavelengths. Some are much shorter, and some are much longer. Physical objects and human bodies vibrate at much lower frequencies than a Soul does. In other words, everything is made up of energy. Our thoughts are also expressed via wavelengths. Any thought not in alignment with either Truth, Joy, Wisdom, or

Love (the purest expressions of the Divine) vibrates at a much lower frequency.

Our ability to tap into our Spirit's connection to Love, Joy, and Wisdom depends upon the vibrational frequency soaring through our instruments, known as our Physical Bodies.

Our bodies resonate with much longer wavelengths when we have many low-vibrational thoughts.

Our physical mind (our brain) is often our focal point for lower vibrational energies and thoughts. Our focal point is where we place our attention. The Soul Star Energy Centre (located approximately 30 cm (1 ft) above our head) and the energy centres above that tend to be our focal point(s) for higher vibrational energies and thoughts.

When our bodies vibrate at much lower frequencies, our attention goes toward our physical mind, where negative-based thoughts tend to arise. It becomes our habit to focus on our worries, what is not good, regrets, fears, money issues, struggles, relationship issues, and everything that is not appearing to go right.

When our bodies are vibrating at much higher frequencies with more positive thoughts, then our ability to focus on the area of the Soul Star Energy Centre is much easier. It is here where we can access Divine Wisdom.

To change the type of energy flowing through us, we need to heal what caused us to become this way. We need to make room for the high vibrational frequencies to come through.

The Law of Free Will means that we have the freedom to choose how we want to live our lives. We have the freedom to live with negativity, and we have the freedom to live with joy. To reunite our connection to our Holy Spirit, we must make a Divine decree to release, grieve, and heal from our past. Once we have done that, we can invite in readiness to show us the way toward a remarkable life.

You see, we are only Beautiful Illumined Beings at our source. I am here to help bring you back to this place where everything becomes magical and mystical—where you can experience joy, creativity, and happiness in your day-to-day life.

Initiation: Making Room for the Inner Goddess

Guided by:
Mother Mary, Jesus, and Serapis Bey

Close your eyes and take a couple of deep breaths. Feel yourself letting go of what you don't need right now.

Imagine yourself connected to Mother Earth. Just feel her warm embrace. Ask her to ground you through this experience.

Know that whatever your experience is, this is perfect for you and Divinely guided by your Inner Goddess.

Mother Mary is coming to you with a soft and very loving presence. She smiles at you and touches your hands. Feel her placing energy into your hands. As she does this, you can feel warm love filling your hands and going to your Sacred Heart. Take some time to feel this moment with Mother Mary.

She says, "I am here to take away all your sorrows. Hand them over to me. Share them with me." You may notice that old feelings are coming to the surface to be released.

Mother Mary wants you to know that you are safe with her. She wants you to know that she understands. She is here, and she is not leaving. She is here to take all the sorrows you have bottled up deep inside you.

Allow yourself to give them to her. Let her be the full expression of a Mother who will nurture you, hold you, and take all your sadness.

FEELING ALONE

Take some time to be in this with her. Feel her blue energy flowing through you.

You can feel yourself being lifted from a heavy weight that has weighed you down. A weight that you feel you carried for far too long.

You can sense how understood you are. Mary knows of all the pain humankind has endured. And she knows it is time to let go and make room for happiness, love, and joy.

Take your time with her as long as you need. You notice that your Sacred Heart has started to make space.

You start to feel complete, and as you do, she moves aside, and you begin to feel the energy of Jesus. Jesus sends his bright, warm yellowish-white light filled with the most Divine Love you could experience, enveloping your whole body.

As you feel this, allow yourself to connect with the truth of Divine Love.

Jesus sends Divine Love softly and warmly into your Sacred Heart, hands, and head. He asks you to feel him.

As you feel him, he gently reconnects you to the Wisdom, Love, and Joy of your Nature.

You have made room for your Inner Goddess to move through you and guide your Sacred Heart, mind, and entire body.

Stay in this energy and experience this sacred reunion with your Inner Goddess and the Love of Jesus.

Before Jesus steps aside, he says, "Know that you can always ask me to reconnect you to your Inner Goddess."

As he steps aside, you feel his Divine Love still filling you.

Serapis Bey comes with a beautiful energy of a luminescent blue. As you invite readiness for this Journey to reunite you with your Inner Goddess, Serapis Bey sends strands of luminescent blue throughout your energy body and physical body.

He is connecting you to the luminescence of the Divine DNA.

Serapis Bey says to you, "Thank You for shining your sweet Soul and embracing humankind with your Love. This luminescence will help your vibration rise to your Divine DNA strands so that you may more easily connect to your Holy Spirit".

Take this moment to notice this Divine Initiation. See yourself make room for readiness for the Invitation of your Goddess to guide you to live a life of meaning and purpose.

Feel this moment. Feel the reconnection to the luminescence within your energy field and physical body.

Mother Mary, Jesus, and Serapis Bey step back and send you a final gift of Love.

They thank you for being ready.

They tell you that you are safe, and they know and acknowledge you for how ready you are.

Take your time to experience this last moment of gratitude and Love they have for you.

Give a prayer of thanks.

Whenever you are ready, you can slowly take a couple of deep breaths, bring your awareness to your eyes and slowly come back.

Reflections

Congratulations on taking this beautiful step of Making Room for the Inner Goddess. You have been initiated into this incredible journey we are about to have together.

Before getting up, take some time to be in this energy. You have had a very high-frequency initiation. While you are in this energy, spend some time journaling your experience. As you journal, you will still be bathing in the warmth and love of Mother Mary, Jesus, and Serapis Bey.

After journaling, spend some time letting this energy integrate into your system. You may feel the effects of it for up to 3 weeks. When you have received such high-frequency energy, it is essential to let your physical body slowly adapt to this shift.

Nurture yourself through this transformation by grounding yourself with healthy foods and walks in nature.

Take your time before moving on to the next chapter.

For now, enjoy spending time integrating and writing your experience in your journal.

HEAL & AWAKEN THE GODDESS WITHIN

FEELING ALONE

HEAL & AWAKEN THE GODDESS WITHIN

CHAPTER 2

RELEASING ANXIETY

"Allow Yourself to Return to Wholeness" - Goddess Sophia

Have you ever caught yourself saying, "my anxiety," as though you own it? Have you ever realized the power you hold in taking ownership of this anxiety you call yours? It was never yours to keep. You are allowed to let it go. In fact, it only showed up for you to ask you to let it go. Let me first explain why it shows up.

Life can be full of challenges. People may hurt us in excruciating ways. We come across situations in life that feel unbearable. After experiencing so many pains, we develop a coping strategy; we start to automatically suppress our feelings so that we don't have to experience our painful emotions so intensely. Over time, this suppression method becomes an unconscious natural method to utilize. After years of unconscious suppression, we wonder why anxiety shows up. And when it does show up, we develop coping mechanisms to handle this anxiety to function. In essence, we hang on to anxiety tightly as though it is a gift to keep and call our own.

You deserve a better life than this. Far better. What if I told you anxiety is a gift, but it is a gift for you to see, honour, and then let go of? Anxiety shows up as your best friend, not your enemy. It is a way of telling your body that you have neglected yourself for far too long.

Anxiety is asking you to check in with yourself to see what you have been suppressing.

Anxiety stems from the word "to choke." What have you been choking within yourself? When we block our feelings due to difficult situations or people, we stop our Souls from being fully expressed. Our Spirit requested that our Soul be housed in this body of ours so that our Spirit can experience the fullest expression of its desires. Our Soul's job is to live out those desires utilizing our body. When our mind is occupied with fear-based thoughts, freedom is taken away from our Soul, and our Soul gets very uncomfortable.

Your Soul communicates to you via your Sacred Heart. Your Sacred Heart is a chakra located between the centre of your chest and throat. From now on, I will call this Energy Centre your Sacred Heart because this is the gateway where you access Divine Love, Wisdom, and Power from your Soul, Holy Spirit and the Divine.

If you are protecting your Sacred Heart from feeling, you won't hear what your Soul is asking of you. Your Soul knows that when push comes to shove, you will listen to your body if you are not listening to your Sacred Heart. This is when your body experiences the constriction of the Soul via anxiety. Your Soul then gifts you with anxiousness being expressed in your body. This is an incredible gift. Isn't it amazing that your Soul can still talk to you even when you aren't listening? It has the power to animate your body so that you can feel physically uncomfortable. This is the only purpose of anxiety. It isn't something you should be controlling or suppressing. Instead, it is a gift to acknowledge and do something about. It is a gift you can honour and then let go of.

So, how do we honour anxiety? Honour and honesty come from the same root meaning. We cannot honour anxiety without being honest with ourselves. When you are honest with yourself, you can be aware of all your hidden (suppressed) needs.

Exercise: Triggers

Preparation for Initiation

Take a moment to think of some situations in your life where you feel triggered (your Soul sends signals to your body to experience anxiety).

1. Write in your journal what bugs you about these situations or people.

2. What is being done or said that makes you feel anxious?

3. What do you feel is being taken away from you at that moment? During anxious times, something IS being taken away from you. Some examples of what can be taken away from you are joy, freedom, self-expression, fun, laughter, having a voice, sensuality (a form of self-expression), love, peace, and happiness. There is an endless list of examples I could give. Take a moment to honour yourself (being completely honest) and write in your journal what is being taken away from you when you feel anxious about a specific situation or person.

Before we continue, I'd like to take a moment to congratulate you for asking yourself how you feel deep down. If you haven't done so yet, I encourage you to take this precious moment to hear the whispers of your Soul. You've got this. Let it all out. Come back here when you are done.

Now that you have taken this time to acknowledge the whispers of your Soul, have you noticed some beautiful feelings about how your Soul would like to express itself through your beautiful vessel called the body?

"If not now, then when?" asks your Soul. Your Soul wants to know when it can come out to play during this time on Earth. How does that feel when I say that to you? For some of you, I can feel the tears coming down. You are a beautiful and precious Spirit, wanting to experience its incredible gifts here on Earth. You have come to this book because you are ready to Awaken so that you can fully express the Holy Spirit.

◆

Exercise: Returning to Wholeness

Preparation for Initiation

Now that you know what has been taken away from you, it is time to invite those qualities back into your life. This is a powerful way to release anxiety from your body. Before starting the initiation, please take a moment to do the following exercise:

1. List each quality that was taken away from you in your journal.

2. Next to each quality, write down what you will start doing to bring that quality back into your life. For example, if you have found yourself in a situation with someone where you felt your voice was being taken from you, what steps can you take now to bring that voice back fully? You may need to have a healthy discussion with someone, letting this person know of your non-negotiables from this point on and that your happiness and freedom are now paramount to experiencing yourself in its fullest expression. In other cases, you may need to let go of

someone to regain your independence. Another example could be that you have found that fun has been taken away from you due to so many stressful circumstances happening in your life. What are you now willing to do to bring fun back into your life?

One significant thing to remember is that these qualities are meant to be experienced throughout your day, not just on weekends or weeknights. This is where the concept of wholeness comes in. To be whole is to invite all of you, all your expressions, into all you do.

Go ahead now, and take a moment to write in your journal each quality that was taken from you and what you will start doing to bring every single one of them back into your life.

Before you begin the initiation, I want to acknowledge you for inviting those qualities back into your life that were taken away from you. I know it takes effort to go back in time and remember those qualities that were stolen from you. Making such an effort means honouring your freedom to have a voice, and it is so important to be able to bring that voice back to the surface again to be heard.

Initiation: Returning to Wholeness

Guided by:
Goddess Sophia and Goddess Diana

Close your eyes and take a couple of deep breaths. Feel yourself letting go of what you don't need right now.

Imagine yourself connected to Mother Earth. Just feel her warm embrace. Ask her to ground you through this experience.

Know that whatever your experience is, this is perfect for you and Divinely guided by your Inner Goddess.

Feel the presence of Beloved Sophia coming down into your space.

She surrounds you with her loving embrace.

Take a moment to feel her love.

Her heart is full of love for you, and she wants to show you how precious and beautiful you are.

She is touching those beautiful words you have written down.

As she touches what has been taken away from you, she lovingly picks up those desires for inner expression and gives them back to you.

She places your Soul's beautiful desires of expression ever so lovingly back into your Sacred Heart.

RELEASING ANXIETY

She then pours cleansing water over your head, washing away all the sorrows you may have felt over time.

She touches your hair and face, cleansing you with this holy water.

You can feel yourself being cleansed back into the purity of who you really are.

You can see as though the water has sparkles, showering you with an incredibly warm, sparkling light.

Sophia invites you to use your hands to scoop up all the parts of you that you left behind. Gently scoop these parts and place them back over your body.

As you do this, you can feel yourself gently bringing back your whole essence.

Feel your Soul smiling.

Your Soul is looking at you with the most sacred love.

Your Beloved Soul thanks you for inviting its desires of expression back into your body.

You deserve this.

Sophia places her hand on your Sacred Heart and tells you how deeply loved you truly are.

She asks you to embrace this love and to allow yourself to experience the wholeness of you.

She says that this wholeness is what you have a right to experience now and forever more.

She says this wholeness is a gift for you to keep.

HEAL & AWAKEN THE GODDESS WITHIN

Everything else, she says, you can let go of.

Breathe deeply in and out and feel yourself inviting wholeness in and letting go of anything that does not serve you.

You are Divine, she says.

Goddess Sophia steps aside as Goddess Diana steps in.

Feel the feminine presence of Goddess Diana.

She comes in with a focus in mind for you.

Her presence is very centred. She is inviting you to feel your mind, Sacred Heart, and body centred into a state of Oneness.

Feel into this Oneness that you are.

Feel all of you. You are complete in all of your perfection.

She invites you to imagine the presence of a Full Moon surrounding you with its beauty and light.

This Full Moon is here to guide you on your path and remind you each month of the wholeness within you.

Allow yourself to give Diana the troubles that held you back from experiencing the full expression of your Soul.

Diana's hands are held open for you to give your troubles to her.

She thanks you.

She bows down to you, honouring you and witnessing what you are ready to let go of.

The Full Moon's energy removes your troubles from Diana's hands.

You watch these troubles get cleansed away, and all that is left is peace, honour, and love.

Diana congratulates you and thanks you once again.

Sophia and Diana come together to remind you of this beauty that you are.

They invite you to go to them anytime to return to wholeness and release what is not whole.

Diana also says you can do this during Full Moons to make it extra special, as the Full Moon is very sacred and is here to serve you.

Take a moment to thank Goddesses Sophia and Diana for this sacred moment together.

Whenever you are ready, you can slowly take a couple of deep breaths, bring your awareness to your eyes and slowly come back.

Reflections

Congratulations on taking this extraordinary step of returning to wholeness and inviting back what was taken from you. You have been initiated into a return to wholeness and a return to your Sacred Spirit's desires.

Before getting up, take some time to be in this energy. You have had a very high-frequency initiation. While you are in this energy, spend some time journaling your experience. As you journal, you will still be bathing in the warmth and love of Goddesses Sophia and Diana.

After journaling, spend some time letting this energy integrate into your system. You may feel the effects of it for up to 3 weeks.

When you have received such high-frequency energy, it is essential to let your physical body slowly adapt to this shift.

Nurture yourself through this transformation by grounding yourself with healthy foods and walks in nature.

Take your time before moving on to the next chapter.

For now, enjoy spending time integrating and writing your experience in your journal.

RELEASING ANXIETY

HEAL & AWAKEN THE GODDESS WITHIN

CHAPTER 3

CLEARING ANCESTRAL TRAUMA

"Let Your Inner Lioness Roar" - Goddess Isis

Your cells are packed full of information. Your body is made up of dancing molecules. These molecules are, in essence, energy vibrating in such a manner to provide you with a solid, physical body. People tend to forget that our bodies are made up of energy. It is not just our Soul and Aura that is in the form of energy. We mustn't forget to acknowledge what is also stored in our bodies energetically. Many people are focused on cleansing the Aura but not fully realizing our bodies are made up of dancing molecules that form our organs, bones, muscles, and tissues, all the way down to our cellular structure.

Energy from the Divine comprises the qualities of Love, Wisdom, and Power. When tapping into this energy from the Source, you will always have access to all three qualities. When in union with this energy from the Source, you will feel a sense of Divine Love. At the same time, you will have access to wisdom teachings and receive guidance while feeling just how powerful and infinite this energy is. This energy also contains the footprint of what has happened before you. Historical information is accessible when understanding how to connect and translate this information you receive from the Divine.

Your cells are vital information senders and receivers. They send information to the brain to tell the brain what it needs to function correctly. The genetic makeup of your cells has been passed on from your ancestors to you. Any unhealed trauma from your ancestors has remained in the cells and has been carried on to you.

You may have felt you have had moments whereby a friend, coworker, or partner says something to you and, suddenly, you get a rush of fear, panic, anxiety, terror, or anger fill you up, and it just doesn't make any sense to you as to why. As a result, you respond in a way that prevents you from feeling more of this feeling. Some protection mechanisms could have resulted in adopting certain behaviours, such as:

* avoiding speaking in public;
* being afraid to give an opinion out of fear of being hurt;
* yelling in complete outrage;
* pretending that everything is okay;
* having the hands, knees, or body shake;
* getting sweaty skin;
* wanting to run away;
* feeling like you are being choked;
* not being able to move or function properly in society;
* suppressing any belief in self and life's Purpose;
* thinking that only intelligent or gifted people can live their life Purpose;
* moving from one relationship to another, finding the same problem;
* feeling like there is no way out, no matter how much therapy you undergo; and
* feeling like there is something wrong with you.

The good news is that there is a way out. You don't have to be experiencing these uncomfortable and debilitating feelings forever. The Divine has gifted you with this cellular memory from your ancestors so that you can free the body and those future generations who are yet to come from these painful memories. The beauty is that you don't have to know what happened in your ancestors' past to release these stored memories.

Exercise: Clearing Ancestral Trauma

Preparation for Initiation

Before your initiation, taking a moment to move your body and get your cellular structure moving is essential. We want to wake up your cells. Before you do that, it is important to first bring into awareness any reactions your body has had in the past.

1. Take a moment to write in your journal all the negative reactions you can ever recall your body having as a protection mechanism to keep you feeling safe. Allow yourself to write freely without any judgements.

Great job! It takes courage to remember and acknowledge any reactions your body has had in your life.

Now it is time to shake up all that stored energy in your body. I recommend you go to an area where you can't be heard. You can put on some music that can help you get moving.

Go ahead and bounce up and down like you are running on the spot. Allow yourself to scream out all the pain you endured from your body, reacting with terror, fear, anxiety, suppression, anger, and other feelings that come to mind. Tell your body that this is all leaving now. Scream it all out. Allow yourself to be the Lion and the Lioness. Roar or scream all of it out and tell your body that all this crap is going away now. Tell your body that the pain is now leaving your bones, muscles, tissues, and cells.

Let yourself bounce up and down and move in twirls or whatever feels right to you. Please do this for as long as it takes until you feel that all the energy is moving in your cells. This may take up to 10 minutes or more.

When you feel complete, take some sips of water, congratulate yourself, and make yourself comfortable to receive the initiation.

Initiation: Clearing Ancestral Trauma

Guided by:
Goddess Isis and the Lyran Realm

Close your eyes and take a couple of deep breaths. Feel yourself letting go of what you don't need right now.

Imagine yourself connected to Mother Earth. Just feel her warm embrace. Ask her to ground you through this experience.

Know that whatever your experience is, this is perfect for you and Divinely guided by your Inner Goddess.

Beloved Goddess Isis steps in and graces you with her presence.

She invites you to feel a balance of Yin and Yang energy moving up and down through your spinal column, into the universe, and through Mother Earth.

As this energy flows through you, you can feel a complete centredness throughout your body and mind.

Using your third eye, she invites you to imagine looking up into the constellations.

As you do this, you see an expansive dark sky filled with bright stars.

She cloaks you with the energy of the Lioness.

Feel yourself resonating with this golden yet powerful Goddess Lioness within you.

HEAL & AWAKEN THE GODDESS WITHIN

See, sense, and imagine this powerful Lioness energy filling you up and expanding outwards into the sky.

Goddess Isis asks you to remain firmly grounded while your Lioness fully expands into the Lyran constellation.

Goddess Isis invites the magical healing properties of the Lyran constellation to enter your cellular being, transforming all lower vibrational memories into the Higher Harmonic of Gold.

This powerful Lioness Energy of Gold transmutes all unconscious, painful ancestral memories, turning them into beautiful golden energy.

You can feel your Inner Lioness empowering herself within you as every cell in your body shimmers in this Gold.

You can feel yourself becoming one with the Power and Beauty of Goddess Isis, feeling the complete balance of your Yin and Yang energy.

Joy overcomes you as you unite with the Power of your Sacred Masculine and the Beauty of your Sacred Feminine.

You can feel your body and mind uniting with all aspects of you.

You can feel yourself uniting with strength, harmony, peace, and inner joy.

Take a moment to send forgiveness to all those who have caused harm to your ancestors.

They, too, shall be released from all connections to your ancestors through the gift of forgiveness.

The Ascended Masters from the Lyran Realm and Goddess Isis invite you to carry this Golden Elixir as a gift within and around your being.

This gift of Golden Light is here for you to remind you of the Sacred Beauty and Incredible Power of the Goddess Lioness within you.

The Lyrans and Goddess Isis thank you for honouring yourself and healing your Ancestral Realm.

Take a moment to thank Goddess Isis and the Lyran Realm for this sacred moment together.

Whenever you are ready, you can slowly take a couple of deep breaths, bring your awareness to your eyes and slowly come back.

Reflections

Congratulations on taking this transformative step of clearing ancestral trauma from your body.

Before getting up, take some time to be in this energy. You have had a very high-frequency initiation. While you are in this energy, spend some time journaling your experience. As you journal, you will still be bathing in the warmth and love of your Inner Lioness, Goddess Isis and the Lyran Realm.

After journaling, spend some time letting this energy integrate into your system. You may feel the effects of it for up to 3 weeks. When you have received such high-frequency energy, it is essential to let your physical body slowly adapt to this shift.

Nurture yourself through this transformation by grounding yourself with healthy foods and walks in nature.

Take your time before moving on to the next chapter.

For now, enjoy spending time integrating and writing your experience in your journal.

CLEARING ANCESTRAL TRAUMA

HEAL & AWAKEN THE GODDESS WITHIN

CHAPTER 4

HONOURING THE SACRED BODY

"Your Body is a Vessel of the Divine" - The Goddess Realm

Have you considered how sacred your body is? Your body has been specifically designed to be a Vessel of the Divine. Without your body, you could not express your Holy Spirit's desires here on Earth. Take a moment to contemplate what this actually means. The Divine gifted you your body to fully express your beautiful Holy Spirit.

How would you welcome the Divine if you knew she was showing up at your doorstep today? What foods would you feed her? Would you help her to feel as comfortable as possible? How deeply would you feel Love for her?

I already know the answer. It would be impossible to give her anything but comfort, love, and gratitude. You would make sure she received the best food possible. You would be in A-W-E of her.

When you mistreat your body, you are saying "No" to the Divine. Let me explain further. Your body comprises thousands of energy channels (also called nadi's). The health of these energy channels is of the utmost importance to allow the vital life force energy of the Divine to flow through us.

The supply of energy from the Divine is infinite. This means that the more open your energy channels are, the more the Divine can flow through them. When piping in water pipes becomes clogged, less water can flow through these pipes. Your body is designed to handle a flow of energy from the Divine that is more than you can imagine. The more you clear your channels, the *more* you will experience the connection to your Holy Spirit. The more you experience this Divine Connection, the more you will Awaken to your Holy Spirit's sacred desires.

Your beautiful energy channels can get clogged physically, mentally, and emotionally. We will first discuss the physical aspect.

Inviting Healthy Foods into the Body

Only foods that come from the Divine were created for your body. The Divine did not create foods processed with pesticides, GMOs, and additives. Those foods were created by humankind for their sacrificial benefit (sacrificing your health for the sake of the illusion of production). These foods create blockages in your body and your energy channels. High vibrational foods must be eaten to allow the Great Flow from the Divine Source. These are pure foods. Your body was not designed to handle chemicals and modified foods.

Your body has a unique barometer system, showing you what feels good to your body and what doesn't. If you have symptoms of feeling happy, peaceful, energized, vibrant, healthy, and clear-headed (no brain fog), your body is telling you those foods are good for you to eat and drink. If you have symptoms of feeling sluggish, tired, unhappy, irritable, or foggy in the brain, then those foods are not healthy for you.

The Goddess Realm would like to remind you to listen to and honour how your body feels. You are naturally designed to experience the Fountain of Youth. This Fountain of Youth is the Eternal Flow of Divine Waters.

Exercise: Inviting Healthy Foods into the Body

Preparation for Initiation

Evaluating the foods you eat is crucial to your mental, physical, and spiritual health. Allow yourself to be the observer with a loving heart. Let go of any judgements, as they do not serve you.

1. Go through your cupboards, pantry, and fridge. Read the labels on the foods. See how many of these foods are modified, processed, and have additives. Journal your findings. What are you discovering?

2. If you don't have food at home and eat out in restaurants, what foods are you buying from restaurants? What ingredients are in those foods?

3. On a scale of 1 to 10, 10 being foods coming directly from the Divine, how would you rate the foods you eat?

4. What foods make you feel energized and healthy? Your body is the best barometer concerning how good a food type is for you.

5. What can you do to bring more Divine foods back into your life?

6. How important is this to you?

I commend you for doing this exercise. Addressing the types of foods one eats is challenging for many people. You did an excellent job honouring your body and being lovingly inquisitive about what foods you are currently eating. Bravo!

Remember to be kind to yourself and know that even one small step can make a massive difference.

◆

Honouring Your Body

Channeled Message Guided by the Goddess Realm

It has been since time immemorial that women were able to honour and love their bodies entirely. There has been such a dis-Grace to the Grace and Beauty of Women. Women have been chastised (beaten), criticized and condemned for being sexual and self-expressive. The goal was sick. The aim was to blame women to the point where they would stifle their Goddess Power. The Goddess has been beaten down into submission with her hands and knees on the ground, having to beg for forgiveness so that she might live.

Women suppressed their voices so that they could feel safe. Generations upon generations have taught women to be quiet. So many women have innately felt afraid to be self-expressive in whatever form that may be. Women were not allowed to be intelligent, emotional, or sexual.

Times have changed, but we are far from where we need to be.

The Realm of Divine Goddesses is gathered here as you read this. They are filling up the room you are in right now. They are all taking a stand for your Inner Goddess no matter what gender you are or identify as. We all have the Goddess archetype within ourselves. The Goddess Realm is here now to assist and empower you in Healing and Awakening the Goddess Within you so that you can fully express your Holy Spirit's desires.

The reason this teaching applies to you no matter what gender you are or identify as is because you will likely have experienced this suppression in many past lifetimes of yours when you were a woman. As a result, many of you will have carried on specific behaviours in this lifetime to keep you feeling protected and safe.

The Divine Goddess Realm would like you to know that your body deserves the freedom to be fully expressed in whatever form you wish. It is time. The time is Now.

Sexual desire is a natural expression of the Holy Spirit and the body. We have this innate desire so we may create and express ourselves. Opening up the Inner Goddess in the body once more allows the awakening of the sacral, creative energy. This is considered sacral because it is, indeed, sacred. The Sacral Energy Centre closes to protect the energy field when fear takes over due to unsafe circumstances. Many people are not aware that they have closed this energy field down.

Being sexually expressive and enjoying your beauty is your birthright. Creativity with sexuality allows you to have the freedom to be sexually uninhibited in the way you choose to be. Many men in this lifetime have closed off access to the creative and expressive part of themselves during sex due to their previous experiences of being suppressed as a woman in past lives. Allow yourself to feel the Sacred Feminine creative energy within you throughout your day. We all have access to these powerful Sacred Feminine qualities within ourselves, no matter what gender we are or identify as. The Divine gave you this powerful gift to harness its beauty, creativity, and strength.

The first step towards re-opening the sacral energy field is to invite the honouring of the body back into your life. Societal norms have been established, telling people what they should look like and how they should behave. You can demand ten orgasms in one day, should you choose. Be the Lioness and the Lion. Allow both the Sacred Feminine and the Sacred Masculine to emerge from you, not just the Sacred Masculine.

Exercise: Honouring Your Body

Preparation for Initiation

It is time to bring back all aspects of you that were told you are not good enough, ugly, fat, skinny, too outspoken, too expressive, too serious, too sexual, not sexual enough, not experienced, naive, too promiscuous, slutty, too emotional, dead, numb, too athletic, not athletic enough, lazy, unfit, etc.

1. Review all your years on Earth and write in your journal things you were told that made you feel less than who you truly wanted to be.

2. Next to those words, write down the opposite, describing who you really are or want to be. If someone told you that you were too noisy, write down the name of the person who said this to you. Next to it, write: I allow myself to be loud, or I honour myself to be loud, or I am free to be loud; in fact, the louder, the better!

   This is a moment to allow yourself to invite all of your incredible qualities back into your life and to honour each part of you, including your sexual vibrancy (don't forget that beautiful part).

Wow! Congratulations! You just did a valuable reflection. Truly. Doing this has massively impacted the healing of yourself and this planet. The Goddess Realm and I thank you from the bottom of our hearts.

Initiation: Honouring Your Body

Guided by:
The Goddess Realm

Close your eyes and take a couple of deep breaths. Feel yourself letting go of what you don't need right now.

Imagine yourself connected to Mother Earth. Just feel her warm embrace. Ask her to ground you through this experience.

Know that whatever your experience is, this is perfect for you and Divinely guided by your Inner Goddess.

The Goddess Realm fills your room with their Divine Feminine presence.

Allow yourself to feel this Powerful Energy.

The Goddess Realm invites you to fill this Goddess Energy inside your Holy body.

As you invite this energy into your body, the area around your pelvis is Awakening.

See, sense, or imagine your Sacral Energy Centre coming to life.

Allow the Vital Force Energy to fill every crevice of your pelvis.

You are Beautiful and Great beyond measure.

Feel movement in your Sacral Energy Centre.

HEAL & AWAKEN THE GODDESS WITHIN

The Goddesses are now gifting you with a symbol in your hands. This symbol represents your freedom to activate your sexual nature, self-expression, and creativity.

Receive the symbol and lovingly place this gift in your belly. This is your sacred symbol, made especially for you.

Feel it activate your sacral area.

Allow yourself to feel the pleasure.

Let your body feel the sense of freedom being activated in your entire body.

As you feel this, you notice the power activated from your sacral area and moves up into your body's energy column.

You can feel the freedom of self-expression empowering your entire body and every cell.

Each cell is vibrantly moving with excitement to express itself freely.

Goddess Isis steps in.

She is the Goddess of complete balance between the full expression of the Creative, Sexual, and Sacred Feminine and the Power of the Active Masculine.

She invites you to feel the Power of the Active Masculine enter your sacral area.

As you do so, you notice the Sacred Sexual Feminine Awaken even more.

A spiral of energy activates upward into your Solar Plexus, bringing forth a Sacred Fire.

This Sacred Fire moves upwards, warming the Sacred Heart.

Sacred, Sexual and Divine Feminine Love emanate from your Sacred Heart into the world.

You invite the feeling of Beauty into your Being.

Feel your body shimmering with the Incredible Divine Goddess within you.

Feel your freedom of expression and right to be you emanate from your entire body.

Feel your entire body coming Alive.

Take some time to feel this Awakening in your Sacred Body.

Your body is a Vessel of the Divine.

Take a moment to thank Goddess Isis and the Goddess Realm for this sacred moment together.

Whenever you are ready, you can slowly take a couple of deep breaths, bring your awareness to your eyes and slowly come back.

Reflections

Congratulations on taking this beautiful step of honouring the Sacred Body.

Before getting up, take some time to be in this energy. You have had a very high-frequency initiation. While you are in this energy, spend some time journaling your experience. As you journal, you will still be bathing in the warmth and love of Goddess Isis and the Goddess Realm.

After journaling, spend some time letting this energy integrate into your system. You may feel the effects of it for up to 3 weeks.

When you have received such high-frequency energy, it is essential to let your physical body slowly adapt to this shift.

Nurture yourself through this transformation by grounding yourself with healthy foods and walks in nature.

Take your time before moving on to the next chapter.

For now, enjoy spending time integrating and writing your experience in your journal.

HONOURING THE SACRED BODY

HEAL & AWAKEN THE GODDESS WITHIN

CHAPTER 5

HEALING THE ILLUSION OF FEAR

"The Key to Eliminating Fear is Letting Go of Resistance" - Goddess Quan Yin

Fear is a predominant illusion people have adopted to call their own. It is unbelievable that people will fight to their death, taking a strong stand for this fear they proudly take full ownership of.

Does this make any sense when you honestly think about it?

What if I told you that the only truth within you is the Love, Wisdom, and Power of the Great Divine?

Why has humanity become inhumane and adopted fear into their lives? Fear has been suckled and nurtured in ways that have destroyed all facets of life. Relationships upon relationships have suffered. Beloved nature has been abused. This tyranny has caused freedom of self-liberation and self-expression to be stunted.

Quan Yin, the Beloved Goddess of Compassion and Mercy, is here to guide you away from this unnecessary entanglement with fear. Quan Yin has vowed to help humanity until they fully liberate themselves from fear and unite with the Holy Spirit.

Now is the time to liberate the Goddess within you so that you can be *entirely* free to be exactly who you desire to be. Are you ready to invite Joy, Health, Love, Creativity, and Passion fully into your life?

There is a key to unlocking the door to freedom from fear. The key is to let go of resistance. When being resistant, the entrance to the Divine closes shut. The opposite of resistance is to allow flow. When we allow, we invite in the flow from the Divine. We invite in the Wisdom from the Divine, along with its Love and Power (Energy Flow and Force). Each cannot exist without the other. This is the science of the Divine.

Therefore, the less the resistance, the more the flow of the Essence of the Divine is moving through you, allowing you to be fully connected to all the Wisdom, Love, and Power you need to manifest the desires of your Holy Spirit.

When realizing that the ONLY truth is this flow and ALL ELSE is an illusion, you are on your way to experiencing a magnificent life. You are meant to live this Magnificence NOW. Not later. Right NOW.

◆

Exercise: Releasing Resistance

Preparation for Initiation & Activation

There are many moments in our day when we invite fear into our lives and are unaware that this moment is an unnecessary moment of illusion. To let go of fear and welcome truth, we must first become aware of all those fearful thoughts we harbour.

Now is the time to make a real commitment to making significant change. Fear is the biggest obstacle that prevents us from experiencing the most extraordinary life possible. Without facing our fearful thoughts and becoming aware of what is possible, we cannot live a fully purposeful life.

Are you ready?

1. Take some time now to think about some days in your personal and professional life. Review the thoughts that are occurring throughout the entire day. In your journal, write your thoughts that are not aligned with the Essence of the Divine (Love, Wisdom, and Power).

    Examples of untrue thoughts are:
    - I will never get what I want;
    - Life is so hard;
    - No one cares about me;
    - Relationships always hold me back;
    - I can never make much money;
    - I'm stuck in the corporate world;
    - I have no choice;
    - I have to be responsible and work hard;
    - I can't speak to him because he puts me down;
    - It's a fantasy for me to live my Purpose;
    - I'm afraid to use my voice;
    - I can't afford good food;
    - I don't have enough time to do what I love;
    - I can't do what that person does;
    - It's too late to start all over;
    - I feel all alone; and
    - I will never have freedom.

2. Next to each of those thoughts you wrote above, write down possibilities that can actually exist for you, next to each untrue belief. Truth comes from a place of Love, Wisdom, and Power.

3. After doing that, spend some time breathing in all the positive possibilities available to you. Potential exists for your desires to come to fruition. The key to manifesting this potential is to remove resistance and allow the Divine to show you the *how*. Your job is to commit to being open and positive to the possibilities that exist for you. Any limiting thought that does not empower you with the Divine Essence of Love, Wisdom, and Power is a lie.

At this moment, you may be thinking, "What about the sad times and the tragedies that occur in the world?" Quan Yin would like you to know that you are correct to say there are moments of grief and terrible moments of tragedy. However, in those moments, you can also allow the Divine to flow forth so that you can feel Love, Wisdom, and Power during that time of tragedy. It is possible to stay connected to the Essence of the Divine.

It is essential to become Awakened and, therefore, *Aware* of your daily thoughts to precisely manifest what the Universe wants to give you.

◆

Well done! This exercise is one of the most important exercises to help you move forward and open yourself up to all the possibilities while you are here on Earth.

Initiation & Activation: Divine Essence of Love, Wisdom, and Power

Guided by:
Goddess Quan Yin and Goddess Emmanuella

Close your eyes and take a couple of deep breaths. Feel yourself letting go of what you don't need right now.

Imagine yourself connected to Mother Earth. Just feel her warm embrace. Ask her to ground you through this experience.

Know that whatever your experience is, this is perfect for you and Divinely guided by your Inner Goddess.

Goddess Quan Yin, Goddess of Mercy and Compassion, fills your Aura and Sacred Heart with emerald green.

Feel her beloved Compassion fill your being.

She tells you she loves you.

The love from her compassionate heart is overflowing towards you.

She invites you to forgive yourself and to be the compassionate person you are for yourself.

Take a moment to feel this compassion and this emerald green energy fill every cell of yours.

She asks you to be aware of all your thoughts with a compassionate heart.

HEAL & AWAKEN THE GODDESS WITHIN

She invites you to transmute all illusionary thoughts into the higher harmonic of gold.

Feel all those negative thoughts you wrote down transmute into golden positive possibilities.

Fill up your Aura and body with this golden light as Goddess Emmanuella steps in.

Goddess Emmanuella is here to bring back your connection to the Essence of the Divine so that you may carry the spark of truth and awareness within you at all times.

Goddess Emmanuella comes in her white gown, moving the energy of gold throughout your Aura.

She is raising your frequency now.

She asks you to smile and feel every part of your body smiling.

Feel your organs, tissues, blood and cells smiling.

They are all smiling because they know you have invited in the purest Essence of the Divine within your body.

"Now is the time," she says.

"You are ready."

Goddess Emmanuella is honoured to provide you with this activation of the Essence of the Divine.

Feel a golden spiral of energy coming down your crown and through your body.

She places a flame of Love, Wisdom, and Power into your Sacred Heart.

HEALING THE ILLUSION OF FEAR

Feel your Sacred Heart warm up.

She is activating the Divine Essence of Love now within your Sacred Heart.

Feel this Essence of Love fill your body with the Divine truth called Love.

"You are Love," Goddess Emmanuella says.

"Let Love guide you.

"Let Love show you the way.

"Let Love remind you of who you really are."

Take a moment to feel this Divine Love emanate from your Divine body.

Goddess Emmanuella now activates the Divine Essence of Wisdom within your Sacred Heart.

Feel this Wisdom grow throughout your body, giving you a feeling of great stillness and being entirely centred.

"You are Wise," Goddess Emmanuella says.

"Allow Wisdom to guide you.

"Allow Wisdom to show you the way.

"Let Wisdom show you all the possibilities that exist for you."

Take a moment to feel this Divine Wisdom emanate from your body.

Goddess Emmanuella now activates the Divine Essence of Power within your Sacred Heart.

HEAL & AWAKEN THE GODDESS WITHIN

Feel your Sacred Heart warm up even more.

Feel this powerful energy grow within your body, revitalizing every single cell.

Feel the Power move and invigorate every part of you.

"You are this Divine Power," Goddess Emmanuella says.

"Let Power empower you.

"Let Power show you your possibilities."

Take a moment to feel this Divine Power emanate from your Divine body.

"Well done, Goddess Emmanuella says," as she smiles with you.

"You have now been activated to the Divine Essence of Love, Wisdom, and Power."

Feel the Essence of Divine Love, Wisdom, and Power fill you up, empower you and guide you now.

Become Aware of this Divine Love, Wisdom, and Power with you always.

Beloved Quan Yin and Goddess Emmanuella invite you to place your hands on your Sacred Heart.

They want you to know that you can come to them whenever you would like to grow the connection to the Essence of the Divine even further.

They seal you with a beautiful spiral of emerald green and gold.

"Namaste," they say to you.

Take a moment to thank Goddess Quan Yin and Goddess Emmanuella for this sacred moment together.

Whenever you are ready, you can slowly take a couple of deep breaths, bring your awareness to your eyes and slowly come back.

Reflections

Congratulations on taking this sacred step of initiating and activating the Essence of Divine Love, Wisdom, and Power within you.

Before getting up, take some time to be in this energy. You have had a very high-frequency initiation and activation. While you are in this energy, spend some time journaling your experience. As you journal, you will still be bathing in the warmth and love of Goddess Quan Yin and Goddess Emmanuella.

After journaling, spend some time letting this energy integrate into your system. You may feel the effects of it for up to 3 weeks. When you have received such high-frequency energy, it is essential to let your physical body slowly adapt to this shift.

Nurture yourself through this transformation by grounding yourself with healthy foods and walks in nature.

Take your time before moving on to the next chapter.

For now, enjoy spending time integrating and writing your experience in your journal.

HEAL & AWAKEN THE GODDESS WITHIN

HEAL & AWAKEN THE GODDESS WITHIN

CHAPTER 6

SHIFTING YOUR FOCUS ON THE DIVINE MIND

"When You Shift Your Focus on The Divine Mind, The Possibilities are Endless" - Lord Lanto

Have you ever heard the saying, "There are 365 days in a year, the equivalent of 52 weeks, 8,760 hours, 525,600 minutes, or 31,536,000 seconds?" Think about that for a moment. There are over 31 million seconds each year. Are you aware of how many thoughts you can have in 1 minute? Too many to count.

The Divine Mind is the aspect of Wisdom that comes from the Divine. When tapping into the Divine Mind, we can quieten our human mind so that we may hear the Wisdom of the Divine. The way to do that is to shift our focus.

We harness our brains' power when we are sitting in our thoughts. When we open our Awareness to the Divine, we harness the power of the Divine Mind.

Our brains are valuable instruments. They have been created to assist us with translating the information that comes from the Divine Mind into a language we understand (e.g. English for English-speaking people). Because the Divine consists of Energy, Wisdom from the Divine Mind is transferred to you via Energy.

All positive creations come from the Divine Mind. Humanity has, more often than not, allowed themselves to be lost in the limited thoughts that occur in the brain. For centuries, humankind has separated themselves from their Awareness of the Divine Mind. This separation has increased the feelings of fear and decreased the feelings of empowerment (bringing in Power (or Energy) from the Divine). People came to believe that all creativity occurs in the brain. Because of this belief, the gateway to the Great Kingdom of Wisdom was accessed less often.

Your brain is designed to translate an infinite amount of Divine Wisdom, should you allow yourself to become *aware* of this Divine Truth.

Now is the time to shift your focus during those 31 million seconds each year towards the Divine Mind. When you shift your focus, you open yourself up to the many possibilities that exist for you. This Earth can provide you with a treasure trove of options when you open up to the Divine Mind.

When you shift your Awareness to the Divine, you open yourself up to your Intuition. Intuition means to look at. People wonder why they don't have the capability of being intuitive. The simple answer is to shift your focus to the Divine. The more you shift your focus toward the Divine, the more you will receive information from the Divine Mind. This is how your intuition opens up.

Awareness is the essential tool that opens you up to the Divine Mind. To be *Aware*, one must be *Awake*. For centuries, people have not even been awake to pay attention to what their minds are focused on. They have let their minds run endless thoughts that do not assist them in aligning with their Purpose. When thoughts are negative, the person is not connecting to the Divine Mind.

When you Awaken yourself by becoming *Aware* of your thinking, you can then remind yourself to shift your Awareness to the Divine. The more you do this, the more you Awaken yourself to your Holy Spirit and your Purpose.

Exercise: Awaken to Your Thoughts

Preparation for Initiation

The first step to becoming Aware of the Divine Mind is to become mindful of how Awake you are of your own thoughts.

1. Take a moment and recall the entire day you had yesterday, from when you woke up to when you went to bed. Try and remember your very first thoughts when you woke up. Write them down in your journal. Then, think about the following primary thoughts you had during the day. Write down all the main thoughts you had throughout your day. As you do this, you can imagine where you were located at the time. This will help you to remember your thoughts.

2. Once you have written them all down, write down next to these thoughts a 'Yes' or a 'No' as to whether these thoughts came from the Divine Mind. If the thought was empowering, it came from the Divine Mind. If the thought was limiting, it came from the brain.

3. Once you have done that, write down on a scale of 1 to 10 how Awake you feel you have been over the past year with where your thoughts have been coming from.

Well done! It takes some effort to go back and remember all those thoughts you had yesterday. Recognizing where you are on a scale of 1 to 10 helps you better understand how to improve your Awareness.

Exercise: Opening Awareness to The Divine Mind

Preparation for Initiation

There are different methods to utilize to open your Awareness to The Divine Mind. I will be sharing with you the various techniques. My recommendation to you is to use a combination of these methods. Using multiple methods allows you to receive information in ways you might not have been able to otherwise.

The first method is to shift your focus from the area inside your head to a location approximately 30 cm (1 foot) above your head. This area is called the Soul Star Energy Centre. The frequency in this area is exponentially higher than the area of your brain. The Divine Mind sends Wisdom to this area. When you focus your mind on this area, pay attention to the following:

- Sensations you are feeling;
- Visions you are receiving;
- Words that are showing up in your brain in the same way thoughts do;
- Inner sounds you may be hearing;
- Scents you may be smelling;
- Any tastes occurring on your tongue; and
- Any sense of inner knowing you may be experiencing.

While experiencing sensations, visions, words (appearing as thoughts in your head), sounds, scents, tastes, or any sense of inner knowing, you can ask, "What does this mean?" You will then get more sensations, visions, words appearing as thoughts in your head, sounds, scents, tastes, or a further sense of inner knowing.

SHIFTING YOUR FOCUS ON THE DIVINE MIND

The answers you receive go to your senses, and your brain helps you to decipher this information into a language you can understand.

1. Take time now to focus on your Soul Star Energy Centre approximately 30 cm (1 foot) above your head. Just place your attention on the area of the Soul Star Energy Centre in the same way you put your attention on your right arm if you were to pay attention to your right arm.

2. Ask the Divine Mind to teach you what you can do to experience Liberation so you can fully live your Purpose. Write down what information you get that can help liberate you to live a life of meaning and purpose. Write freely in your journal what comes to you and trust in the process. During the act of trusting, you learn to receive great teachings from within.

Congratulations! Doing those exercises requires effort because you may be utilizing a part of yourself in a way you don't often do. Some of you may feel an energetic shift, experiencing a higher frequency of energy entering your body, or you may experience one of your energy centres opening up. This is a normal part of the process.

It is important to ground yourself whenever you do energy work. The more you get grounded, the better you can house the Holy Spirit within your body. This way, you can better decipher the information you receive from the Divine Mind. When you are not grounded, your body will tend to feel too vibrationally 'high.' When this occurs, it is difficult for the brain to translate the energy into a language you can understand. The best way to ground yourself is to spend time with Mother Earth daily by eating healthy foods and walking in nature. The more you ground yourself, the more embodiment of the Holy Spirit you can experience in your body.

Initiation: Opening Awareness to The Divine Mind

Guided by:
Lord Lanto

Close your eyes and take a couple of deep breaths. Feel yourself letting go of what you don't need right now.

Imagine yourself connected to Mother Earth. Just feel her warm embrace. Ask her to ground you through this experience.

Know that whatever your experience is, this is perfect for you and Divinely guided by your Inner Goddess.

Beloved Lord Lanto enters your energy field.

A beautiful bright, and soothing yellow energy fills your Aura.

Lord Lanto takes your hand and places a gold necklace in your hand.

You take this gold necklace and place it around your neck.

On the end of a necklace is a pendant designed especially for you.

You can feel this pendant resting right at your Sacred Heart.

Beloved Goddess Isis steps in and places a symbol over your third eye on your forehead.

This symbol on your third eye area keeps you balanced and centred during your connection with the Divine Mind.

Goddess Isis steps away, and Lord Lanto continues with you.

SHIFTING YOUR FOCUS ON THE DIVINE MIND

Lord Lanto places a mantle of yellowish gold in your Sacred Heart.

This mantle extends vertically and horizontally from your Sacred Heart.

The resonance of your body is shifting to the resonance of the Divine Mind.

Lord Lanto is aligning you with the Gateway to the Divine Mind, where you can access Divine Wisdom.

You feel this mantle of yellowish gold extending from above and below your Sacred Heart, past your feet and head and into the Universe.

You also feel this mantle of yellowish gold extending from your Sacred Heart's left and right sides, moving across your arms and into the Universe.

You experience the Gateway to the Divine Mind opening up even more.

Take some time to experience this sacred moment.

"You are a Sacred Holy Spirit," Lord Lanto says.

He says, "The time has come to initiate you into the Awakening of your Connection to the Divine Mind.

"You are here for a Purpose, and that Purpose is granted to you.

"You are now Awakened to this Golden Ray of the Divine Mind.

"You are empowered with this Golden Ray so that you may live your Purpose."

Lord Lanto thanks you for taking this empowering step in Awakening yourself to the Divine Mind.

"The Golden Ray is incredibly grateful to you for uniting with Divine Wisdom," Lord Lanto says

"You are Blessed."

Lord Lanto thanks you again as he seals your Aura with a golden symbol.

Take a moment to thank Lord Lanto for this sacred moment together.

Whenever you are ready, you can slowly take a couple of deep breaths, bring your awareness to your eyes and slowly come back.

Reflections

Congratulations on taking this significant step of Opening Awareness to the Divine Mind.

Before getting up, take some time to be in this energy. You have had a very high-frequency initiation. While you are in this energy, spend some time journaling your experience. As you journal, you will still be bathing in the warmth and love of Lord Lanto.

After journaling, spend some time letting this energy integrate into your system. You may feel the effects of it for up to 3 weeks. When you have received such high-frequency energy, it is essential to let your physical body slowly adapt to this shift.

Nurture yourself through this transformation by grounding yourself with healthy foods and walks in nature.

Take your time before moving on to the next chapter.

Enjoy spending time integrating and writing your experience in your journal.

SHIFTING YOUR FOCUS ON THE DIVINE MIND

HEAL & AWAKEN THE GODDESS WITHIN

CHAPTER 7

REMOVING STRESSORS FROM YOUR LIFE

"Invite Self-Compassion in your Life so you can Awaken to Your Divine Passion" - Goddess Quan Yin

Your body is a Sacred Signalling System telling you when your mind is going astray. When your body experiences tension, this tension acts as a signaller to let you know that too many stressors are occurring in your life. When we don't listen to these signals, dis-ease occurs in the form of anxiety, stress, and physical and mental health issues.

When you honour your body's signals, you connect to the Divine Goddess within, who shares her feelings with you. At the same time, you are honouring your Holy Spirit's calling, as your Holy Spirit is forever guiding you back on track so that you may live your Sacred Purpose.

People have learned how to become so busy in their lives. They have taken on the responsibilities of the world, often trying to help others in so many ways. The challenge with this approach is that they often don't have time for themselves anymore. They have lost their connection to their Divine Spark.

People have become so busy with being busy and feel they can handle it all. Do you feel at peace with everything you do? Do you find yourself, frequently, at war with yourself, convincing yourself to make time to do "one more thing"?

When you are busy, do you feel that you are always in the flow and connected to the Divine? Can you feel this Divine energy flowing through you at all times?

The goal here is to experience this Divine energy filling you up and flowing through you in everything you do.

When you honour your body and spend a moment to connect with your Sacred Heart, you will soon see what your Holy Spirit is longing for. But this can only happen when you have time for yourself to be able to listen.

The medicine for stress is to eliminate the stressor. Period.

People feel they cannot live peacefully because they have so many responsibilities, resulting in little time for themselves. I am here to tell you that this is a fear-based illusion. Since the Divine has granted you free will, why not use it to your advantage?

The more stressors you invite into your life, the less you experience flow, love, joy, happiness, and the Wisdom of the Divine.

The only way to Awaken to and live your Purpose is to stay plugged into Source Energy.

It is time to break free of these chains we have wrapped around us.

You deserve to experience more flow, movement, peace, tranquillity, joy, and enthusiasm.

It is time to invite self-compassion into your life so that you can Awaken to your Divine Passion. When you take time to care for yourself, you can more easily listen to your heart and its needs.

When we become overtaken by stress, this means we, most certainly, did not fully listen to what our heart had been telling us before the pressure arrived. We operated from the Limited Mind, telling ourselves what we "have to do."

When we direct our attention to our Sacred Heart and the Divine Mind, we can allow the solutions to all our problems to be shown.

When we focus on our Limited Mind, we tell our body to get very busy, not trusting that the Divine Mind will easily provide many solutions.

The only responsibility you have is to direct your attention to the Divine Mind, honour the needs of your Divine Vessel (your body), and act according to the Wisdom of The Divine, expressing itself through your Sacred Heart. When you hang out in your Limited Mind, you allow your mind to create more stressors.

It is impossible to Awaken to and live your Purpose when you are succumbed to stress.

Now is the time to let that stress go.

◆

Exercise: Letting go of Stressors

Preparation for Initiation & Activation

1. Take some time now to consider all the activities that you are currently involved in. Make a list of each activity in your journal.

2. Next to each activity, write down on a scale of 1-10 (1=no stress and 10=highest stress) how stressful each activity feels to you. Before you place a rating, check in with your body rather than your mind as to what the rating should be. A way to do this is to put your hand on your Sacred Heart, close your eyes, take a couple of deep breaths and then think about that activity. Think of the activity and ask your body what the rating *feels* like on a scale of 1 to 10. Your body knows best.

3. After reviewing your list, using the signaller of your body again, determine which Top 5 items from that list rank as the highest stressors in your life.

4. Use your body signaller again from those Top 5 items to pick 3 of them that you are willing to shift. When you choose them, do not worry about the *how* because the Divine Mind will help you to figure this out.

5. Next, connect with the Divine Mind in the area of the Soul Star Energy Centre, and, using *only* your intuition, ask what methods you can utilize to eliminate these Top 3 stressors from your life. Pay attention to sensations, visuals, words (expressed as thoughts), scents, tastes, anything you might hear, or any instant inner knowing you will get. Be open to whatever answer might come. Allow the answer to be different than what you *think* it may be. From my experience, most often, the solutions given to me are entirely different than what my Limited Mind thought of as a solution. So, please allow yourself to experiment with the Greater Divine Mind and let it guide you. Write down what the Divine Mind has told you to do to eliminate these Top 3 stressors from your life.

◆

Well done! You have honoured the Goddess Within. Listening to your body's signaller and the Divine Mind allows you to eliminate stressors and Awaken to your Divine Passions.

Please also remember that you accessed very high-frequency energy by focusing on the Soul Star Energy Centre. It is always important to ground yourself whenever you do energy work. This way, you can better decipher the information you receive from the Divine Mind.

Initiation & Activation: Awakening to Your Divine Passions

Guided by:
Goddess Quan Yin and Archangel Raphael

Close your eyes and take a couple of deep breaths. Feel yourself letting go of what you don't need right now.

Imagine yourself connected to Mother Earth. Just feel her warm embrace. Ask her to ground you through this experience.

Know that whatever your experience is, this is perfect for you and Divinely guided by your Inner Goddess.

Feel the energy of Beloved Quan Yin fill your Aura.

Take a moment to feel this emerald green energy and her compassion envelop you.

Beloved Quan Yin asks you to place your hands on your Sacred Heart.

She invites you to feel a warm, compassionate love emanate from your hands.

Quan Yin places her hands on your Sacred Heart and asks you to feel compassionate forgiveness enter your being.

Forgive yourself, she says.

Forgive yourself for all the wrongdoings you have placed upon yourself.

HEAL & AWAKEN THE GODDESS WITHIN

Know that you did the best you could at the time.

Feel the flow of forgiveness fill your Sacred Heart.

Now, she says, you are ready for guidance so that you may take the next steps on your path with ease.

Beloved Quan Yin now asks you to invite ease into your life.

Feel the energy of ease fill your Aura and body.

As this energy of ease fills your body, Archangel Raphael enters.

Archangel Raphael is the Healing Archangel.

You feel swirls of bright green energy wrap around your Aura.

You feel old burdens releasing from your cells, tissues, muscles, organs, and entire mind and body.

You can feel these burdens being cleansed from your Aura.

Archangel Raphael is here to cleanse and consecrate you in the immaculate conception of your Divine Passions.

Quan Yin says, "You must make room, sweet Soul, so you can invite the consecration of your Divine Passions to enter this world."

"Your mind and body must resonate with your Divine Spirit so that you may house your Holy Spirit in your body."

Archangel Raphael and Beloved Quan Yin bless you now.

Feel this blessing swirl around your entire being.

You are now being consecrated into the Awakening of your Divine Passions.

Spend some time now experiencing this consecration with Archangel Raphael and Beloved Quan Yin.

"You are Holy," Beloved Quan Yin says.

Feel yourself uniting to the Wholeness that is You.

Goddess Quan Yin and Archangel Raphael thank you for taking this time to release what no longer serves you and making room to invite your Purpose and Passions into your life.

They invite you to go to them whenever you need healing and blessings.

They are always here for you to heal and guide you on your wonderful journey of empowerment.

Take a moment to thank Goddess Quan Yin and Archangel Raphael for this sacred moment together.

Whenever you are ready, you can slowly take a couple of deep breaths, bring your awareness to your eyes and slowly come back.

Reflections

Congratulations on taking this sacred step of Awakening to your Divine Passions. This was an initiation and activation to open up your Awareness pathway toward your Divine Passions.

Before getting up, take some time to be in this energy. You have had a very high-frequency initiation. While you are in this energy, spend some time journaling your experience. As you journal, you will still be bathing in the warmth and love of Beloved Quan Yin and Archangel Raphael.

After journaling, spend some time letting this energy integrate into your system. You may feel the effects of it for up to 3 weeks. When you have received such high-frequency energy, it is essential to let your physical body slowly adapt to this shift.

Nurture yourself through this transformation by grounding yourself with healthy foods and walks in nature.

Take your time before moving on to the next chapter.

For now, enjoy spending time integrating and writing your experience in your journal.

REMOVING STRESSORS FROM YOUR LIFE

HEAL & AWAKEN THE GODDESS WITHIN

CHAPTER 8

EMBRACING YOUR DIVINE PASSIONS

"Your Divine Passions are Lying Inside of You Ready to Become Awakened" - Beloved Mary Magdalene

Did you know your passions are resting inside of you? For some, they are still lying dormant, ready to become Awakened. Many people are not aware of their passions and Divine Purpose. I have heard so many people say:

- How do I find my Purpose?
- How do I find my passions?
- Is there such a thing as having passions or a Purpose?
- Do people really have a Purpose?
- How can I feel my passions?
- How do I connect with the heart?

Do you see a common theme? People think that passions are somewhere to be found, as though they are somewhere out there.

We have lost connection to what is real. We have lost contact with the freedom that lies within. We can't see our passions because we have closed the gates to our freedom. We tend to think that freedom involves escaping and having the freedom to run. But the reality is that freedom lies within. It is the freedom that so many are running from.

When you can s-l-o-w down, you can feel your passions come to the surface. Slowing down allows you to hear. Imagine running through the woods, listening to your feet stomping as you run. When you take a moment to stop, suddenly, you hear the birds in the distance and the tiny creatures moving all around the trees and the forest floor. When you take a moment to stop and listen in the middle of the woods, your sense of peace heightens. You can feel a calmness enter your being. When this happens, you notice your body feeling so free.

You see, it is in the stillness where freedom and peace envelop you. It is also in this stillness that you feel your passions emerge. During those moments of calm, you can remember all those creative times you have had when you felt the most content. People underestimate the many moments of creativity that occur in their lives. The act of being creative has often been limited to the arts. Because it has often been limited to the arts, many people have closed the doors to realizing their own incredible creative abilities.

You are a mighty creator and have brought endless creations to the world. The root word of "create" is "to grow." There are so many examples I can give that involve growth. When you speak, you are creating. You are adding ideas to this planet. You are sharing your pearls of wisdom. You are helping others to grow by bringing in this wisdom from the Divine Mind. When you rest in front of others, showing them the peace that can be involved in relaxing, you teach others the beauty of relaxing. You teach others what they can uncover while resting. When you eat while being present, you teach others how to be present while eating. You teach them to be mindful and experience the glory of the Divine by eating with mindfulness (being aware of the Divine Wisdom, Love and Power that exists within). When you breathe with awareness, you teach others to be mindful of their breathing and experience this loving energy flowing through them. When you share what you see, you teach others to see all the beauty around them. All these simple examples exemplify the act of creation. You create from your passions.

Your passions can be as simple as those given above. What is it you love to do or love to be? Identifying your passions involves going within and listening to your sweet Soul's experiences. What has your Soul loved doing or being? Millions of examples can be given that are unique to each individual. Some examples of passions are:

- Being at peace. Does being at peace move you to the core and make you wish so many others could experience peace?
- Sharing with family. Do you feel such a deep connection when having a strong family bond that you wish others could experience this type of connection?
- Seeing other children joyfully playing. Do you wish you could help children to experience joy in their daily lives?
- Eating incredible food. Do you feel so invigorated when you eat certain foods that you wish others could connect to these types of foods so that they, too, could feel invigorated?
- Dancing and movement. Do you love the art of dancing and experiencing the movement of the Holy Spirit through dance? Would you love others to feel this pleasure as well?
- Having healthy skin. Have you seen others struggle with healthy skin and wish you could share with them all the techniques you know to have healthy skin?
- Singing. Have you experienced liberation with singing, even though you are not a gifted singer? Do you wish others could experience this liberation even if they don't have natural singing voices?

- ❖ Enjoying the taste of food. Have you experienced pleasurable and unique sensations through tasting specific foods? Do you wish others could awaken their senses and enjoy food's glory?

- ❖ Being mindful. Have you benefitted from being mindful that you wish to help others with this skill so they can become more aware of all the available possibilities?

As you can see, there are many ways to experience passion. I could write thousands upon thousands of examples. What do you feel sparks your interest when you tap into your Soul? It just takes one passion that can ignite your Purpose in life. One passion alone.

Take the example of being mindful. If this was someone's greatest passion, they could spend their entire life teaching others how to become experts on being mindful. This would be an incredible skill to offer. This could change millions of lives for the better. People would learn how to experience joy by learning to become mindful of making better life choices.

The key to discovering your passion is getting as quiet and still as possible so you can hear the simplicity of your passion. Uncovering this simplicity enables you to create abundant joy for others, including yourself, and you will live out your passion with Purpose. Wouldn't this be amazing?

Now is the time for the world to wake up to their Spirit's desires. Your Soul has come here to animate your Holy Spirit's desires through your Divine Vessel (the body).

◆

Exercise: Becoming Aware of Your Passions

Preparation for Initiation & Activation

1. Spend some time now connecting to the stillness within you, right within your Sacred Heart. Place your hands on your Sacred

Heart, activate the mantle of the Golden Ray from Lord Lanto, stemming from your Sacred Heart and extending vertically and horizontally from it, opening the Gateway to the Divine Mind. Feel this peaceful energy envelop you and bring you into the stillness of the Divine Spirit in your Sacred Heart. Spend some time experiencing this sacred stillness.

2. Allow your Holy Spirit to *Awaken* your memories of moments in your life when you felt sparks of passion. Write in your journal each spark that comes to your awareness.

3. Let yourself feel each spark of passion. Write each passion you identify in your journal and what moved you during those specific memories. Let the expressions be as simple as possible. When you uncover the simplicity of your feelings, you can better experience the strength of this particular passion embodying you.

4. Next to each spark of passion, write down what you wish the world could experience regarding this particular passion.

5. Once you have listed all these sparks of passion, connect with the Divine Mind and Sacred Heart to rate each on a scale of 1-10, with 10 being the strongest passion.

6. Identify your Top 3 passions from the list you have created.

Wonderful! By connecting with this beautiful energy, you have activated your Divine Passions. Congratulate yourself for taking the time to remember this vital part of you—your Holy Spirit's desires.

Initiation & Activation: Embodying Your Divine Passions

Guided by:
Beloved Mary Magdalene

Close your eyes and take a couple of deep breaths. Feel yourself letting go of what you don't need right now.

Imagine yourself connected to Mother Earth. Just feel her warm embrace. Ask her to ground you through this experience.

Know that whatever your experience is, this is perfect for you and Divinely guided by your Inner Goddess.

Beloved Goddess Mary Magdalene approaches you with her lovely yellow Aura centred with a pink flame.

You can feel her Aura meld with yours.

Your Sacred Heart begins to be activated with the pink flame.

Mary Magdalene says to you, "This pink flame is forever yours. It activates access to your Divine Love and, hence, your Divine Passion.

"For it is your Divine Passion that stems from your Divine Love.

"You see, it is Divine Love who needs to create.

"And, from this Divine Love, your Passions are Born."

Feel your Passions activating within your body now.

EMBRACING YOUR DIVINE PASSIONS

Feel your Aura pulsing and radiating this Divine Golden Wisdom Flame and the Divine Love Flame stemming from your Sacred Heart.

You are becoming the radiant sceptre of the Divine.

Feel this sceptre radiate from all aspects of your being.

You are now embodying your Divine Passions.

Feel them emanate from every precious cell of yours, activating all parts of your body.

You are now carrying the torch of your steadfast Divine Passions.

"Hold this torch with pride," Mary Magdalene says.

See yourself walking with this torch as though you are a part of an Olympic ceremony.

You are marching at this ceremony to Awaken the masses with your incredible Passions so that they, too, can live joyous lives.

Feel the audience smiling and eagerly wanting to experience a piece of your brilliance.

Feel the tears of joy.

"You are meant to experience this Magnificence of you now," Mary Magdalene says.

"I am here for you always.

"I am here to spread your wings.

"I am here to help you Awaken humanity so humanity can fly.

"You are on a precipice of a New Age. And that New Age is Now my beloved Shepherd.

"I love you."

Mary Magdalene points to the stillness in your Sacred Heart.

It is there where all the answers lie.

"Go within," she says.

"It is there where I shall lie.

"It is there where I shall dance alongside you.

"I will be the flame of your inspiration.

"Whenever you call upon me.

"Eternally, I am yours.

"Forever in Gratitude.

"I AM."

Take a moment to thank Goddess Mary Magdalene for this sacred moment together.

Whenever you are ready, you can slowly take a couple of deep breaths, bring your awareness to your eyes and slowly come back.

Reflections

Congratulations on taking this beautiful step of embodying your Divine Passions. This was an initiation and activation to the Gateway of Divine Love, where all your Passions are born.

Before getting up, take some time to be in this energy. You have had a very high-frequency initiation. While you are in this energy, spend some time journaling your experience. As you journal, you will still be bathing in the warmth and love of Beloved Mary Magdalene.

After journaling, spend some time letting this energy integrate into your system. You may feel the effects of it for up to 3 weeks. When you have received such high-frequency energy, it is essential to let your physical body slowly adapt to this shift.

Nurture yourself through this transformation by grounding yourself with healthy foods and walks in nature.

Take your time before moving on to the next chapter.

For now, enjoy spending time integrating and writing your experience in your journal.

HEAL & AWAKEN THE GODDESS WITHIN

EMBRACING YOUR DIVINE PASSIONS

HEAL & AWAKEN THE GODDESS WITHIN

CHAPTER 9

AWAKENING TO YOUR DIVINE STRENGTHS

"Your Divine Spirit is Ready for You to Live Your Ultimate Purpose" - Goddess Peddamma

Like strands of a rope that have been twined together to create its incredible strength, your Soul has undergone a journey of lifetimes, taking a strand from each life to make this rope of yours. This rope is inherently unique, representing the distinctive strengths you have chosen to develop in each lifetime.

Do you ever wonder why you are naturally gifted at something? It just comes so easily for you, yet it doesn't come so easily for others. We tend to take for granted these gifts we inherited from our past lives.

These strands of yours are strengths that your Soul has developed because your Holy Spirit would like its Purpose manifested while utilizing these strengths. Suppose your Holy Spirit's Purpose was to be a speaker worldwide and make a significant change in the political environment so that there would be unified peace in the world. In that case, the strength that would have been developed over lifetimes is the ability to communicate highly effectively.

Each lifetime builds upon the previous one, so your Divine Spirit can live and fulfill its ultimate Purpose.

You have come here to read this book because your Holy Spirit is ready to live its ultimate Purpose. Your Spirit has been preparing you for this moment. Your time is nigh. You are ready. All you need to do is remember those strands you have developed so that you can twine these strands with your Divine Passions and create your unbreakable rope.

◆

Exercise: Becoming Aware of Your Strengths

Preparation for Initiation & Activation

As previously said, we take our strengths for granted, as they seem normal to us. To twine these strengths with your Divine Passions, you must become aware of your valuable strengths.

1. Take a moment to review your life. Allow yourself to get centred into your Sacred Heart and connect with the Divine Mind at the Soul Star Energy Centre. Go back to when you were a child and review the years up until now.

2. Write in your journal what people said they appreciated and admired about you and what they thought you were good at.

◆

Exercise: Becoming Aware of Your Strengths From Past Lives

Preparation for Initiation & Activation

Now that you have activated your energy field to go into remembrance mode, you will now go deeper. You are about to access the strengths you developed from your Past Lives. You may be wondering how this is possible. It is simpler than you think.

When you are connected to the Divine Mind, you have access to all parts of you, including all the memories from your Soul's encounters over the years.

1. Centre yourself back in your Sacred Heart. Keep feeling the Divine Energy in this area while placing your awareness on the Divine Mind at your Soul Star Energy Centre.

2. Ask the Divine Mind to show you what strengths you developed in your past lives. Pay attention to the images and intuitive sensations that now enter your awareness.

3. Write in your journal the strengths that are being shown to you. Some of you may end up receiving detailed information from some of your past lives. You can also take some time now to write those details down.

Please note that some of you may not get details of what occurred in past lives. Know that you are being shown what you are meant to see. With all intuitive work, trusting in the Universe is vital. It is always essential to let go and trust. Trust that you will be shown at the right time what you need to know. All you need to do is listen and be aware. For today's exercise, it could be that the sole information you receive consists of images and feelings regarding your strengths. Trust in the process and let yourself have fun.

Well done! You have just done massive work! You have reawakened yourself to all of your impressive past accomplishments. You deserved to take that moment to acknowledge all that you have done to create your unique strengths.

Please remember that whenever you access the Divine Mind, you access an incredibly high frequency. Grounding with good foods and walks in nature helps to integrate this energy fully.

Initiation & Activation: Twining Your Rope of Divine Passions with Your Divine Strengths

Guided by:
Mary Magdalene and Goddess Peddamma

Close your eyes and take a couple of deep breaths. Feel yourself letting go of what you don't need right now.

Imagine yourself connected to Mother Earth. Just feel her warm embrace. Ask her to ground you through this experience.

Know that whatever your experience is, this is perfect for you and Divinely guided by your Inner Goddess.

Feel the presence of Goddess Peddamma stepping in and greeting you.

I am here, she says.

You can feel her incredible sacred gold and grounding brown Aura emanate from her being.

It is I who have come to slay the demons that are holding you back from living your full potential.

Imagine all those self-limiting beliefs lifting off your Aura and moving towards Goddess Peddamma.

She takes out her golden sword and slays all those demons in front of you.

You can see all those self-limiting beliefs completely vanish with her golden sword.

HEAL & AWAKEN THE GODDESS WITHIN

The room is now filling up with an incredible golden light.

Goddess Peddamma takes her Divine Golden Sword and holds it over your head.

Liquid gold drops drip from her sword and enter your Crown Energy Centre.

You can feel this liquid gold enter your Crown and move down your energetic spinal column.

You can feel this liquid gold begin to spiral.

Goddess Peddamma is now connecting with all of your past lives.

See her taking every individual strand from each past life and twining each strand into a Divine Rope in your energy column.

You can feel your Divine Golden Rope getting stronger and stronger.

It is so stunning.

You can feel your rope extend from your spinal column up to your Divine Holy Spirit.

Goddess Peddamma smiles at you and tells you how proud of you she is.

She puts her hands in a prayer position and says, "Namaste."

Mary Magdalene steps in.

Feel her golden pink Aura envelop your being.

Mary activates your Passionate Heart.

"Have you ever wondered why it is called a Passionate Heart"?

AWAKENING TO YOUR DIVINE STRENGTHS

"It is here where your passions dwell."

"It is here where I dwell," as she places her hand on your Sacred Heart.

Feel this beautiful connection with Mary Magdalene at your Sacred Heart.

Feel the Passionate Pink Energy from your Sacred Heart begin to flow and twine with the Golden Divine Rope in your energy column.

You can see your Divine Rope shimmering in gold and pink strands.

Feel your Passions being activated by your Divine Strengths.

"It is your Divine Strengths that fuel your Passions to Live," both Mary Magdalene and Goddess Peddamma say.

Feel your Divine Strengths covet your Divine Passions.

"You are powerful beyond measure," Goddess Peddamma says.

"Become one with this Pink and Golden Treasure of yours."

You can feel your Holy Spirit climb down your strong, passionate pink and golden rope.

You can feel your Holy Spirit uniting with you now.

Feel and immerse yourself in her Divine Goddess Presence.

"You are one with me," she says.

Feel her Divine Love, Passion, and Strength.

Goddess Peddamma, Mary Magdalene and your Holy Spirit place a Pink and Golden Pyramid of Protection all around you.

HEAL & AWAKEN THE GODDESS WITHIN

This is your sacred vehicle.

This is your inner sanctity.

This is where you can go to experience and witness your Divine Purpose unfolding.

This is where all your creations will be built.

Take a moment to feel the energy of being in your Pink and Golden Pyramid with the Pink and Golden Rope extending from your spinal column to your Holy Spirit.

Feel your Passions and Strengths Awakening to their fullest potential.

Feel your creativities expanding.

"You are so ready," they say.

Mary Magdalene and Goddess Peddamma encourage you to invoke this Sacred Pink & Golden Pyramid around your Aura daily. You may connect with them anytime you need guidance on your Divine Strengths and Passions.

In this Sacred Pyramid, you can access and explore all of your Divine Creativities.

Take a moment to thank Beloved Mary Magdalene, Goddess Peddamma, and your Holy Spirit for this sacred moment together.

Whenever you are ready, you can slowly take a couple of deep breaths, bring your awareness to your eyes and slowly come back.

Reflections

Congratulations on taking this significant step of twining your Divine Passions with your Divine Strengths. This was an initiation and activation of twining your Divine Strengths with your Divine Passions.

Before getting up, take some time to be in this energy. You have had a very high-frequency initiation. While you are in this energy, spend some time journaling your experience. As you journal, you will still be bathing in the warmth and love of Beloved Mary Magdalene and Goddess Peddamma.

Mary Magdalene and Goddess Peddamma encourage you to invoke this Sacred Pink & Golden Pyramid around your Aura daily, with the Pink and Golden Rope extending from your spinal column to your Holy Spirit. You may connect with them anytime to help steer you on your path. In this Sacred Pyramid, you can access and explore your Divine Creativities.

After journaling, spend some time letting this energy integrate into your system. You may feel the effects of it for up to 3 weeks. When you have received such high-frequency energy, it is essential to let your physical body slowly adapt to this shift.

Nurture yourself through this transformation by grounding yourself with healthy foods and walks in nature.

Take your time before moving on to the next chapter.

For now, enjoy spending time integrating and writing your experience in your journal.

HEAL & AWAKEN THE GODDESS WITHIN

CHAPTER 10

MAPPING OUT YOUR DIVINE PURPOSE

"The time has come to Trumpet the Horn" - Goddess Athena

You have come very far! You have reconnected with your Divine Strengths and Passions. Bravo! Now is the time to unite these qualities and form them into possibilities. There are a plethora of options awaiting you. Now is the time to unfold these Divine Strengths and Passions and create your incredible Divine Purpose Map. This map of yours unveils your Divine Purpose. Let us begin.

Have you ever heard of the terminology "to Brainstorm"? Brainstorming is the act of mind-mapping possibilities, whereby all options are written down. No possibility goes unnoticed. If the thought occurred, it gets written down. There is no right or wrong answer during brainstorming. All ideas are welcome during a brainstorming session. During group brainstorming sessions, it is clearly understood that no one is to be judged. This is how it works in corporate brainstorming sessions. Once the ideas have been listed, the group rates these possibilities to determine which would make the most sense to follow up on.

You will do something similar, but, in this case, you will connect with your Passionate Heart and Divine Mind to receive guidance. We will be calling this heartstorming. I am calling this heartstorming because you will get away from what your brain thinks you "should" be doing. You will also be getting away from "doing what makes sense." Remember, the brain is of a very Limited Mind. One of the purposes of your brain is to help you decipher what comes from the Divine Mind, where possibilities are endless.

Your Holy Spirit knows all the answers and what is best for you. We have closed down the sacred door to our Holy Spirit for years. Now is the time to reopen that door, so we can, once and for all, hear our Spirit's Sacred Divine Decree to live our Purpose fully.

You came to Gaia for a reason. This reason was to experience a plentitude of your imaginations coming into fruition in the here and now.

Goddess Athena is here to take a stand for everyone to wake up, stand tall, and tear off the illusion of fear. Athena commands you to "boldly become the amazing person you always wanted to FULLY BE." "The time is now," she says. "NOW."

◆

Exercise: Heartstorming

Preparation for Divine Purpose Mapping

It is time for some incredible yet Super Powerful Heartstorming! Now that you have identified your Divine Strengths from this life and your past lives, along with having discovered your Divine Passions, you will heartstorm possibilities of what you can do with these Divine Strengths and Passions of yours to create a life of Purpose and meaning. Remember that with heartstorming, there is no wrong answer. Every answer is to be honoured and encouraged as a possibility.

Go back and grab the lists you have written out of your Divine Passions and Strengths. Have them handy so that you can see them in front of you. You will map out many ideas of how each strength can fuel a passion.

The same method applies if you map out a Personal or Business Purpose. Your business purpose is likened to a Personal Purpose, as your business represents you and what you truly want to manifest in this world.

I will first give you some examples to better understand the various options you can create for living out your Divine Purpose.

Mary's Divine Passions (to name a few) are:

- Creativity through art—wishing the world could be fully expressed;
- Cooking—wishing the world would experience more joy in gatherings, sharing in a common value; and
- Listening—wishing the world would take some time to listen to the delightful stories people have to share with what makes them uniquely them.

Mary's Divine Strengths (to name a few) are:

- Being an artist;
- Being a great cook;
- Being a fantastic listener;
- Excellent at connecting women together;
- Being an amazing Mom;
- Plays Cello well; and
- Being a heart-centred person.

Heartstorming out the Possibilities Above of how Mary could live out her Personal Purpose or Business Purpose:

- Connecting women together in gatherings, helping them to open up their Sacred Heart;

- During these gatherings, the Cello could be played, and teachings could be taught on how to open up the heart while listening to the Cello;

- Skills could be learned on how to listen to the Cello with the heart. These women may not realize how busy their minds are. Mary could teach them the nuances of how individual notes play off of each other to form subtle expressions that personify certain emotions;

- Another gathering could involve teaching women to use a paintbrush and some paint and guiding them to listen to the strokes they are painting and hear what their heart has to say to them via each brush stroke;

- Another possibility could be to teach moms how to connect with their hearts and better listen to their children. Some moms may have lost the heart connection with themselves, thus having lost the heart connection with their children;

- A gathering could be done where children and moms would learn how to prepare food together, and the skills could be taught on how to listen to each other's desires; and

- The cello could be played, and the mom learns how to listen to what the child experiences while listening to the cello. The child shares what she experiences.

As you can see, the possibilities could keep going on and on from the example above. If the above were a business, the marketing message would consistently be targeted towards helping women open their hearts to those who have felt they have closed them down. The end result is to open women's hearts so they can enjoy being in community with others, sharing their hearts and feeling beautiful, strong connections.

1. Now, it is your time to have some fun! Go ahead and do some Heartstorming, laying out all the fantastic possibilities you could create. Remember that there is no wrong answer, and the point of this exercise is to generate as many ideas as possible until you entirely run out of ideas. The example I gave above is just a tiny portion of the number of ideas that could be created.

   So, go ahead now and list all the potential possibilities that could be created with your Divine Strengths fueling your Divine Passions. If you can, allow yourself to write pages worth of possibilities in your journal. This is your opportunity to dream, so allow yourself to dream big.

You did it! Hats off to you! Isn't it incredible what possibilities exist for you? You took the time to honour yourself fully, and I commend you for that. Very few people have taken the time to connect with their Sacred Heart to hear what their Spirit wants them to experience on Gaia.

Exercise: Mapping Out Your Divine Purpose

Preparation for Initiation

Now that you have heartstormed, review the list above and write out which ideas appeal to you the most. It is here where you will create a Map of your Divine Purpose.

In the example of Mary I gave above, one scenario could be that Mary prefers to work only with women rather than with children. In this case, she would focus solely on helping women open their hearts.

The second scenario of Mary could be that Mary wants to only focus on opening women's hearts to children, and the sole focus would be on that instead.

1. Take a moment to connect with the Golden Ray of Lord Lanto and the Pink Ray of Mary Magdalene. Feel your Sacred Heart connect you to the Divine Mind and your Passionate Heart. Feel yourself sitting in the Pink and Golden Pyramid with the beautiful golden rope connected to your Holy Spirit. Allow your Divine Spirit to climb down this rope and spend time with you in your Sacred Pyramid.

2. As you are immersed in this sacred connection, Map out your Divine Purpose by writing in your journal which ideas from your heartstorming session felt most aligned with your Holy Spirit's Divine Desires and your Purpose.

You did it! Truly commendable! You had the most sacred journey possible, connecting to your Divine Spirit and listening to your Holy Spirit's sparks of wisdom, love, and encouragement as your Holy Spirit showed you the way toward living your Divine Purpose.

Initiation: Celebration of Awakening to Your Divine Purpose

Guided by:
Goddesses Athena and Mary Magdalene

Close your eyes and take a couple of deep breaths. Feel yourself letting go of what you don't need right now.

Imagine yourself connected to Mother Earth. Just feel her warm embrace. Ask her to ground you through this experience.

Know that whatever your experience is, this is perfect for you and Divinely guided by your Inner Goddess.

Powerful Goddess Athena steps in as she trumpets her horn in celebration of your Victory!

Feel the incredible Power of Goddess Athena's stature and strength as she hovers over you in sheer gladness and joy.

Her very bright yellow Aura saturates you with her presence.

Take a moment to feel this incredible, powerful presence of Goddess Athena.

"I have come to show you The Way."

"I have come to show you The Light."

"I have come to show you the Brilliance that you are."

"Declare to yourself, "I AM Brilliant!"

"Feel this Brilliance of yours emanate from the Core of your Being."

HEAL & AWAKEN THE GODDESS WITHIN

Athena sounds the trumpet once more.

She says out loud for the world to hear, "I AM announcing the birth of this Brilliant Master. This Master is here to help Awaken Humanity. Let this Beloved Divine Presence be a Torch to you all."

Feel Athena taking you by the arm and walking you along the stage, celebrating your Divine Manifestation amongst the crowds of millions of people.

They all look at you in awe.

"You are this greatness that the entire crowd sees," she says.

"Take this in, for it is mightily earned."

She blows the horn once more.

Hear the crowd cheering.

"It is you they are celebrating," she says.

"This is no small feat. I stand tall next to you, so very proud of what you have produced as you birthed your Holy Spirit's right."

As you stand there amongst the crowd, cheering you on, they start singing you a victorious song.

Tears of joy fall from your face.

This is such a beautiful, sacred moment.

You have reached the pinnacle of this Fountain of Youth of yours.

This Fountain is here to stay.

Let it flow wherever your feet touch the Earth.

MAPPING OUT YOUR DIVINE PURPOSE

Take a seat on the stage and spend some time receiving this appreciation for all that you have become.

As you take in the appreciation, Goddess Mary Magdalene and Goddess Athena stand in front of you, yet to your sides. Together, they lift their golden swords in the air and mark the celebration as they touch their swords together in front of you.

As their swords touch in front of you, golden energy enters your Sacred Heart and fills your body and Aura.

You are now being initiated into communion with your Divine Purpose.

Feel this precious energy from Goddesses Athena and Mary Magdalene as they stand firmly by your side, fully protecting you, so that you may live out your Purpose with gusto.

Goddess Athena places golden bracelets on your wrists.

"You are now initiated into the Inner Sanctity of the Divine Feminine, where your mighty Purpose stands fulfilled.

"We shall forever be by your side, witnessing your Brilliance unfold and reach heights you have not yet seen.

"We are one with you as you are one with us.

"Take my Strength and Mary Magdalene's Passion and make them your own.

"Fight for your right as a Spirit Purpose Warrior to shine your Brilliance upon humankind.

"Make it so.

"And so it is."

Feel Athena's Divine Strength as a Goddess Warrior and Mary Magdalene's Divine Passion envelop you now.

Allow yourself to integrate this energy, feeling yourself become one with it.

Goddess Athena and Mary Magdalene bless you and thank you for attending your Joyous Celebration.

Take a moment to give thanks to Beloved Goddesses Athena and Mary Magdalene.

See them holding hands, smiling at you.

Whenever you are ready, you can slowly take a couple of deep breaths, bring your awareness to your eyes and slowly come back.

Reflections

What a joyous, sacred, and powerful celebration that was for you! You have been initiated into the Inner Sanctity of the Divine Feminine, where your Holy Spirit's Purpose is expressed. Allow yourself to be the Spirit Purpose Warrior, fighting for your right to live out your Divine Purpose.

Before getting up, take some time to be in this energy. You have had a very high-frequency initiation. While you are in this energy, spend some time journaling your experience. As you journal, you will still be bathing in the warmth and love of Goddess Athena and Beloved Mary Magdalene.

After journaling, spend some time letting this energy integrate into your system. You may feel the effects of it for up to 3 weeks. When you have received such high-frequency energy, it is essential to let your physical body slowly adapt to this shift.

Nurture yourself through this transformation by grounding yourself with healthy foods and walks in nature.

Take your time before moving on to the next chapter.

For now, enjoy spending time integrating and writing your experience in your journal.

MAPPING OUT YOUR DIVINE PURPOSE

HEAL & AWAKEN THE GODDESS WITHIN

CHAPTER 11

EMBRACING YOUR DIVINE POWER

"To experience Greatness manifesting in our lives, we must align with that Greatness" - The Divine

The world is your oyster. I'm sure you have heard of that saying, but have you honestly contemplated the depth of this phrase? Imagine looking down at a precious pearl created within an oyster shell. This beautiful pearl is a metaphor for your life. You can transform any situation into a magical pearl.

Now that you have formed your Divine Purpose into a magical idea, it is time to believe, empower, and create this idea into a Divine Pearl.

Some of you may think that the possibility of manifesting your Divine Purpose is far away from you. You may feel it is a dream that will take a long time to manifest. While I understand what you are feeling, Goddess Athena wants you to know that this thought is an illusion. This thought is not reality.

Before I begin explaining, I want to share with you that we, as humans, all get in our own way. We are in a constant growth process. All of us face the struggle of deciphering illusion from reality.

So, when I share with you the guidance that is about to come through me, I'd like you to know that this wisdom applies to every person, including myself.

When you think something will take a long time to manifest, it will because you just thought that. What you think ends up manifesting. When you believe that things take time to manifest, then they will. Feeling and thinking go hand in hand.

Understanding the Science of Divine Will and Divine Motion is paramount to fully understanding the Universe's Power. Divine Will is omnipresent. It is always here. Divine Will is the *answer* to your questions. Divine Will gives you the *result* of everything you think, regardless of whether your thoughts are positive or negative.

This means that how you think you are, you, therefore, are. In essence, Divine Will is *always* present and *always* acting. You have free will to manifest whatever it is you wish. Divine Will always responds immediately in likeness. When you think you are not healthy, you are not healthy. When you believe it will take a long time to thrive, it will take a long time.

The Source always provides what you *will* into your life. It is impossible for Divine Will not to respond because Divine Will is always present and acting. To experience Greatness manifesting in your life, you must align with that Greatness.

You are One with the Divine. You are born as a Creator. This is a difficult concept to fully recognize as humans because this concept can feel scary to many. To understand that you have access to this Greatness is incredible. Your Greatness is dependent upon how you experience the Divine Greatness within you. As above, so below.

The *moment* you *know* incredible possibilities are manifesting in your life, the Universe has *already* responded. This response sets in Divine Motion all the resources you need to experience these creations of yours.

Deeply understanding the Power and Science of Divine Will means that what you align with, you receive. When you align with lack, you receive lack. When you align with problems, you receive issues. Immediately. There is no time delay. The Power of

Manifestation lies within your ability to align with what you truly want.

The fundamental principle to experiencing manifestation is to align with your inner *knowing*. When you align with your inner *knowing*, you know that what you want is already at your doorstep. You don't need to worry about the *how* because the *how* is already there within Divine Will. Divine Will *is* the *how*.

When you realize this potential within you, you can fully understand that you are the Creator of your Reality.

This means that you can live your Divine Purpose *now*. The answer and resources are already existing in Divine Will. You only need to align with your Divine Purpose. I do not say this lightly, as I know what it takes to shift my mindset. It may not be easy, but it is well worth it.

All you need to do is create new neural pathways and strengthen the use of positive thoughts and feelings. When these positive neural pathways are strengthened, you will develop new habits of thinking and being. You will start to see possibilities everywhere. You will manifest what others think impossible to achieve into the possible. You will align with the Mind of the Divine. You will align with Greatness, and answers will be most evident in your life. You will see solutions everywhere.

Exercise: Aligning with Your Divine Purpose

Preparation for Initiation & Activation

You will now do what most people do not do when they strongly desire to change their lives. You will address that part of you that has created limited thinking concerning how you can fully manifest your Purpose in life.

Remember that your outside environment reflects the world you are living in on the inside.

1. Take some time to write in your journal all the challenges you feel regarding living your Divine Purpose *now*. What limiting thoughts or feelings arise?

   Examples of limiting thoughts are:
   * I don't have enough money;
   * I am not educated;
   * It will take a long time; and
   * I have too many other responsibilities.

   The Law of Divine Will responds to each of those thoughts above with likeness. When you are aligned with the Power of the Creator within you, you will realize just how important it is to align with the *positive* Power of Creation. Until you do, life in front of you will have many limitations. When you do align with this incredible Power of the Creator within you, infinite possibilities exist for you *now*.

   Allow yourself to list every challenging thought and feeling that comes up for you about your Divine Purpose Map.

2. After creating that list, create a new list of possibilities that are actually available for you when you align with your incredible Divine Purpose.

3. What new thoughts and feelings do you need to create to align with these great possibilities that exist before you?

4. Do you want to manifest your Divine Purpose *now*? What inner *knowing* do you need to align with to manifest this Divine Purpose *now*?

   For example, if you feel it will take a long time to earn money and manifest your dream, then it will take a long time to make money. In this case, the inner *knowing* you would need to align with is that your vision is already in manifestation, and you only need to allow it to happen. You don't need to know the *how*. When you align with the inner *knowing* that it is already in existence, the Divine Mind will show you the *how*. For example, in this case, the *how* could manifest in some of these ways:

   * Someone comes into your life who has lots of resources and wants to assist you in manifesting your Divine Purpose;
   * You can find a way to get a loan, and you discover how to get a quick return on investment;
   * You discover a speedy way to earn the money you need;
   * You find cash; or
   * You realize an alternative solution that doesn't require additional money.

   Go ahead and write in your journal all the challenges and mindsets you need to shift to align with receiving *positive* manifestations of Divine Will.

Congratulations! What you have done is epic! You understand Divine Will's fundamental Power and Principle and have just set your Divine Purpose in Divine Motion.

The key to keeping your Divine Purpose in Divine Motion is to stay aligned with the *positive* thoughts and feelings within you. Feel these phenomenal possibilities that exist within you during your every moment.

Initiation & Activation: Aligning with the Power of Divine Will

Guided by:
The Divine and your Holy Spirit

Close your eyes and take a couple of deep breaths. Feel yourself letting go of what you don't need right now.

Imagine yourself connected to Mother Earth. Just feel her warm embrace. Ask her to ground you through this experience.

Know that whatever your experience is, this is perfect for you and Divinely guided by your Inner Goddess.

Activate the Sacred Pink and Golden Pyramid all around you.

Feel the golden mantle of Divine Wisdom activated in your Sacred Heart and aligned with the Divine Mind.

Activate the pink passion flame of Divine Love in your Sacred Heart.

Feel yourself sitting in the centre of your Sacred Pyramid.

Your Holy Spirit climbs down your Divine Rope and joins you now.

Feel the Divine Presence of your Holy Spirit.

Awaken your Sacred Heart and Divine Mind to the joyful possibilities within you as you live out your Divine Purpose Now.

Feel these possibilities merging with your body.

Feel the Joy, Love, and Passion emanate from your being.

See your Holy Spirit invigorated and dancing with glee.

You are manifesting your Divine Purpose Now.

Feel this manifestation fill your Sacred Pyramid.

Feel the expansiveness of your Divine Purpose vibrating in every molecule around you and in your Sacred Pyramid.

Feel yourself aligning with Divine Will now.

Feel Divine Will responding back with Joy, Love, and Passion.

Merge with this Mighty presence of the Divine responding to you with Joy, Love, and Passion.

Allow this Divine Joy, Love, and Passion to fill your being and expand outward to the world.

Invite the inner knowing that your Divine Purpose is manifesting through you now.

Feel the inner knowing that Divine Will is responding to your resonance.

You are one with the Divine.

Experience this Power of your Oneness with the Divine.

Experience this Power of your Oneness with Divine Will.

Feel yourself centred in Joy, where all solutions are present.

See yourself letting go of the old, limited you.

See yourself setting yourself free to limitless possibilities.

See yourself soaring into the Universe, experiencing the full Greatness you are.

EMBRACING YOUR DIVINE POWER

It is here, in this realization, that you are fully aligned with Divine Will.

Take some time to experience this complete alignment.

You are One with this Greatness.

You are One with Divine Will.

All your answers are fully supplied.

For it is here where there are no questions.

It is here where you have the power to align with what is.

You are fully aligned with your Divine Purpose.

See yourself now connecting to the Divine Mind.

Experience the Wisdom of the Great Divine Mind now.

Feel this Wisdom and inner knowing envelop you.

You are one with Divine Wisdom and inner knowing.

It is here where you are fully embracing your Divine Power.

Feel your Divine Power soar through you.

Feel yourself one with Divine Power.

Feel this Divine Power fill up your Sacred Pyramid.

You have the power to manifest your Purpose now.

You are one with Divine Love, Wisdom, and Power.

Feel the Divine Essence flame activate from your Sacred Heart now.

Experience this Divine Essence of Love, Wisdom, and Power rise into your Aura and fill your Sacred Pyramid.

Feel the expansiveness of your Sacred Holy Spirit within you, emanating and rising as Divine Love, Wisdom, and Power.

I AM THAT I AM

Take a moment to give thanks to the Divine and your Holy Spirit.

Whenever you are ready, you can slowly take a couple of deep breaths, bring your awareness to your eyes and slowly come back.

Reflections

No words can fully describe what being one with the Divine and the Holy Spirit is like. You have received an alignment with Divine Will and have been initiated into your Divine Purpose. The Essence of Divine Love, Wisdom, and Power has been more profoundly activated within you.

Before getting up, take some time to be in this energy. You have had a very high-frequency initiation and activation. While you are in this energy, spend some time journaling your experience. As you journal, you will still be bathing in the warmth and love of the Divine and your Holy Spirit.

After journaling, spend some time letting this energy integrate into your system. You may feel the effects of it for up to 3 weeks. When you have received such high-frequency energy, it is essential to let your physical body slowly adapt to this shift.

Nurture yourself through this transformation by grounding yourself with healthy foods and walks in nature.

Take your time before moving on to the next chapter.

For now, enjoy spending time integrating and writing your experience in your journal.

EMBRACING YOUR DIVINE POWER

HEAL & AWAKEN THE GODDESS WITHIN

CHAPTER 12

CALLING FORTH THE ACTION TAKER WITHIN YOU

"Allow Yourself to Soar to Great Heights" - Eagle Spirit

You have made incredible strides towards Healing and Awakening the Goddess Within so that you can discover your Purpose. Hats off to you! Truly! Now that you have Awakened and Aligned to your Purpose, you can move forward by taking the steps necessary to live your Divine Purpose.

I'm sure you have heard the saying, "Analysis Paralysis." Have you already found yourself analyzing things ad infinitum once you discovered your Divine Purpose? Let me first begin by saying that you are not alone. Most people have developed this pattern of thinking.

Esoterically speaking, being in analysis paralysis is not a natural way of being. Your Divine Spirit is the essence of who you are. When you align with the nature of your Divine Spirit, there is no need for analysis paralysis; you can be in the flow and take action on the guidance that naturally comes your way.

The sole reason we analyze things to death is that we are terrified that something might go wrong.

Now is the time to jump into the air like a young eagle for the first time, and trust that you will learn how to fly and soar with the wind during that first moment of falling.

The number one thing that will keep you away from living out your Divine Purpose is living in fear. Keeping busy with analyzing is what can keep people stuck for a lifetime. Keeping busy gives people the illusion that they are actually doing something.

The action takers are the young eagles who first hop from branch to branch on one of the tallest trees to gain balance. And then, they do it—they leap off and trust in the wind to take them to heights they had not yet conceived.

You are now ready to take that leap of faith. When you take that leap of faith, you align with the inner *knowing* that the Law of Divine Will responds immediately to your action. When the young eagle takes its first leap, the wind responds and lifts the eagle as the eagle uses its wings to work with the wind. The eagle *knew* that the wind would respond and that the *how* would be revealed.

When living your Divine Purpose, you have invited your Holy Spirit to animate your Soul in your Divine Vessel (the body). It is impossible to *fully* live your Divine Purpose using the Limited Mind. This is why understanding that Goal Setting does not always work when the Goal Setting is created with the Limited Mind.

The trick is to get out of your Limited Mind's way and align with Divine Will and the Divine Mind, receive the guidance necessary, and take the leap of faith.

In this discovery, you will find that mistakes will *appear* to be made along the way. What actually occurs is that you discover what you need to do to make something even better than it was previously. You reach the point of discovery whereby you realize that you are ready for the next teaching that will enable you to achieve even greater heights. In this moment of realization, there is an opportunity to experience immense gratitude and excitement for this new revelation.

So, what you perceive as failure is actually an opportunity for you to learn how to use your wings even better to handle the fiercest wind and use it to your advantage to rise to greater heights.

Are you ready to soar?

Now is the time. Now.

◆

Exercise: Discovering the Actions You Can Take

Preparation for Initiation

Now is the time to get out of the logical mind. Your next steps can only be revealed via the Divine Mind. It is first essential to understand the Law of Reality. Time does not exist in reality. When I discuss reality, I'm referring to the essence of the Divine. The only reality is the energy of the Divine and its creation: your Holy Spirit. This creation is always existing. The Divine is ever-present. Once you are born, your physical body and mind experience time and space.

When you allow your Divine Purpose to be revealed, you connect to the Divine and your Holy Spirit where there is no time and space. It is here where you receive guidance. This guidance comes from your inner *knowing*. This guidance comes from the Divine Mind. Understanding this concept is key to unlocking the guidance that already exists within you.

Now is the time to discover the next steps you can take toward living your Divine Purpose. Understand that the guidance you receive in this realm will not show you a linear, sequential path. I need to explain this in Sacred Geometrical terms for you to understand this concept fully.

Wholeness represents a Circle in Sacred Geometry. The Divine is Whole. The Divine represents Oneness (also known as The One). It does *not* symbolize a line. A line represents time. Time is only present in the 3D world here on Earth. When your body dies, you no longer experience time because you are no longer in your body. When you leave your body, your experience of Oneness is ever-present.

The Presence of the Divine *only* exists in the Now. Because a circle represents Wholeness, it also represents existence only in the Now, where all answers and results occur. Divine guidance comes from The One as the essence of a Circle, esoterically speaking. This means you will not be taking logical, sequential action steps that the Limited Mind is so used to understanding.

Divine Will is ever-present in the Now. Our job is to align with that which is already present. I will now share with you how to receive guidance from the Divine regarding the next steps you are to take to live your Divine Purpose.

Imagine dividing up a circle into 12 segments, as you would with a pie chart, and colouring each segment a different colour. Even though the pie chart is separated into 12 different coloured sections, a whole circle is still present. This is how the Divine Guidance on what action steps to take towards living out your Divine Purpose unfolds. You may first receive guidance on the 3rd sector, then the 7th sector, then the 12th sector, then the 1st sector, and so on. As you can see in this analogy, there is no linear path.

When you do goal setting using the Limited Mind, there will be many more challenges and limitations ahead of you because you are not entirely in alignment with the Divine Mind and your Holy Spirit.

Some guidance you receive from the Divine Mind will not make complete sense to you. Remember that when you are operating in the esoteric realm, the Law of Divine Reality, you are working in the Now—in the Wholeness—in the Circle.

You must be the young eagle, have faith, and align with the inner *knowing* that you will fly.

When you align to this inner *knowing*, Divine Will must respond. Make your alignment great, so Divine Will can respond to the greatness you have aligned with, allowing you to soar to great heights.

1. Take a moment now to connect with the Divine and your Holy Spirit. Activate your Sacred Pyramid and feel this beautiful golden and pink energy fill it up. Witness your Holy Spirit climbing down your Sacred Rope and meeting you. Connect to the Divine Mind to receive the guidance given to you by your Holy Spirit. Ask what steps to be taken next. This is Divine Goal Setting. Write in your journal the steps you are given.

   Trust in *knowing* that you are being shown the sectors of the circle that you are meant to see now. It is here where there is no need for analysis.

2. Start doing the steps you listed above. Make sure you allow yourself to have fun doing them.

3. When you have completed those steps (which may take days or even months to fulfill), come back and do this exercise again to receive Divine Guidance on the next steps you need to take toward living your Divine Purpose. You will be coming back to this exercise throughout your life to receive Divine Guidance in all that you want to do.

   Trust in the experiences that will be occurring for you while taking action steps. *Know* that these experiences will help you soar to greater heights.

   I have sometimes taken actions that felt like I was going backwards or taking too giant of a leap ahead. Afterward, I realized how perfectly that moved me toward living my Divine Purpose and how brilliant it was to experience that.

   Trust in the process and know that all is Divinely guided.

♦

You are brilliant! I commend you for doing what very few people on this planet are doing. It takes courage to trust this new process and go against societal norms.

I honour the eagle within you. I am witnessing you soar to majestic heights. What a blessing!

Initiation: Soaring with the Divine Eagle Within You

Guided by:
Eagle Spirit

Close your eyes and take a couple of deep breaths. Feel yourself letting go of what you don't need right now.

Imagine yourself connected to Mother Earth. Just feel her warm embrace. Ask her to ground you through this experience.

Know that whatever your experience is, this is perfect for you and Divinely guided by your Inner Goddess.

Feel yourself standing at the top of the Grand Canyon on a warm sunny day.

You can feel your skin so pleasantly warm from the Golden Sun.

You see the beauty of the red rock surrounding you.

Your heart opens up to this incredible vista.

You feel loved by the beauty that Beloved Gaia has blessed you with.

You see beautiful Condors and Eagles flying above in the far distance.

You see them soaring so majestically.

This beauty captures your Holy Spirit.

HEAL & AWAKEN THE GODDESS WITHIN

You feel your Holy Spirit climbing down to meet you to experience this magnificent beauty with you.

You feel your Holy Spirit within you slowly raising your Holy Spirit arms and taking on the shape of an Eagle.

You feel your entire Aura in the shape of an Eagle.

You look up and see Eagle Spirit coming down from above, landing ever so majestically in front of you on this beautiful red mountain.

Feel the powerful presence of Eagle Spirit.

Eagle Spirit has a message to give you now.

Take some time to receive this Divine message from Eagle Spirit.

Eagle Spirit then looks out to the Grand Canyon and says, "You are Ready."

"Come with me."

Eagle Spirit leaps up and lets the wind take him as you see him majestically fly into the beauty of the Grand Canyon.

Now is the time for you to join Eagle Spirit.

You feel your body, mind, and heart enveloped with faith.

You can feel Divine Knowledge enter your Soul.

Your Soul knows the wind will take you and show you the way.

With complete trust, you feel yourself leap into the air and off you go, soaring into the beautiful Grand Canyon.

CALLING FORTH THE ACTION TAKER WITHIN YOU

You are entirely free, experiencing the greatness of this moment with Eagle Spirit guiding you to unique places that cannot be seen with the human eye.

Take some time to experience this vast beauty.

Eagle Spirit brings you back to land on the spot where you started from.

Eagle Spirit touches your third eye and initiates you into the reunion with your Divine Eagle Spirit.

Feel Eagle Spirit blessing you now.

You have been initiated into the Divine Eagle Kingdom.

It is here where you may soar to great heights.

Eagle Spirit tells you your Divine Eagle Spirit may fly with him whenever you please.

It is where you may join the Holy Spirit Condors and Eagles in their Sacred Flight.

Your body fills with deep love, joy, excitement, and wonder.

Eagle Spirit blesses you once more and gives thanks.

Take a moment to give thanks to Eagle Spirit.

Eagle Spirit flies away.

Your heart has been filled with a deep connection with Eagle Spirit that will last a lifetime.

You take a moment in silence, witnessing this feeling and the majestic beauty around you.

Whenever you are ready, you can slowly take a couple of deep breaths, bring your awareness to your eyes and slowly come back.

Reflections

You have received a very sacred blessing and initiation from Eagle Spirit. You are truly blessed that Eagle Spirit has come to initiate you into his Kingdom.

Before getting up, take some time to be in this energy. You have had a very high-frequency initiation and activation. While you are in this energy, spend some time journaling your experience. As you journal, you will still be bathing in the warmth and love of Eagle Spirit and your Divine Eagle Spirit.

After journaling, spend some time letting this energy integrate into your system. You may feel the effects of it for up to 3 weeks. When you have received such high-frequency energy, it is essential to let your physical body slowly adapt to this shift.

Nurture yourself through this transformation by grounding yourself with healthy foods and walks in nature.

Take your time before moving on to the next chapter.

For now, enjoy spending time integrating and writing your experience in your journal.

CALLING FORTH THE ACTION TAKER WITHIN YOU

HEAL & AWAKEN THE GODDESS WITHIN

CHAPTER 13

ALIGNING WITH POSITIVELY DRIVEN PEOPLE

"When the wind is not in your sail, you must tack against the wind" - Goddess Daphne

It is of utmost importance to keep aligned with your goal to maintain a consistent direction. There will be times when the wind is not in your sail. During those times, you will need to know how to tack against the wind to continue your journey and reach that targeted goal.

Life is meant to be experienced with loved ones. Loved ones include acquaintances as well. So, when I refer to loved ones, I'm referring to anyone who embodies love as a significant part of their daily lives.

When we have lull moments, it is often helpful to talk to a loved one to receive encouragement to continue on our incredible purpose-driven path.

You have done tremendous work with Healing and Awakening the Goddess Within. This work is not something all those you know can relate to. Many people you currently know may still be living with many fear-based realities; turning to them could result in receiving a fear-based response from them.

This means that if you turn to them and share your incredible purpose-driven ideas, you may not get the response you want. You may be filled with many adverse reactions, discouraging you from taking those significant steps. It is not because they don't care about you. They care so much about you that they would be willing to fight with a sword to help you not go down a path *they* feel will lead you to treachery. I say this with an expression of agony because that is how they believe things will occur for you. They will be experiencing triggers that will invite fears to arise from trauma held down in the cellular.

It is vital to understand whom you are speaking to and to be kindly aware of what they are ready to handle. If they are not open to healing, they will likely not be receptive to your ideas for your new life.

This can feel disheartening to many. I understand. Everyone makes a choice, and that is their choice to make. Just remember that you, too, have a choice. What I'm about to share with you is that there is brilliance awaiting alongside your preferences.

So what do you do? The answer is simple. Tack until you find new loved ones who can put the wind in your sail. While you tack, you are experiencing a forward momentum towards your end goal. You will be able to taste the satisfaction on your lips from learning how to tack so cleverly against the wind and maintain your targeted direction.

I am not saying to let go of old loved ones, although some of you may want to and may choose to. I am suggesting that you become aware of the mindset that some of your loved ones are in. Steer toward those who maintain a consistently positive attitude. These are the people who will help you toward living your greatness. It is these people who believe that your possibilities will be manifested.

Through trial and error, I have learned whom I should not speak to.

When you reorient yourself and tack upwind, you will discover many outstanding, new people who may be even more advanced on the path than you are right now. These people already *know* how manifestation works because they are living examples of it. These people can also see positivity through any challenge. They fully comprehend that when a "failure" has occurred, an opportunity has arisen for them to understand what is not working. These people are grateful for "failures." In fact, they expect them. But they don't describe them as "failures." They see them as opportunities for improvement. I would add that failures are opportunities to understand further the best solutions that align with your purpose-driven life.

Lastly, I recommend you err on the side of caution as to whom you choose to speak your Sacred Holy Spirit's Purpose and desires. Your Purpose is sacred and can only be revealed by you. Remember what their mindset is. Love them for who they are. Try not to fight them, for they are at their own growth stage. It can be extremely frightening to hear whenever a desire to live a Sacred Purpose is revealed to people not living their Purpose. They think you are not living in reality. They believe life is hard and that it is impossible to do what you really love doing in life. You will hear, "You have to be *responsible!*" That will be a hard pill to swallow. It doesn't have to be a pill you must take.

Think about all those people ahead of you who are living their Purpose and pinching themselves in the joy of doing this. They took responsibility for believing in themselves and took whatever action was necessary to *ensure* they would live the life of their dreams.

That is what you deserve. Wholeheartedly and truly.

Exercise: Becoming Aware of Whom You are Aligned With

Preparation for Initiation

1. Take some time now to become aware of the mindset of your loved ones (including acquaintances). We tend not to let ourselves be aware. We often see our loved ones for who they are deep down inside. We tend not to pay attention to how they see themselves.

   Make a list of these people and write in your journal on a level of 1-10 how ready you feel they are to wholeheartedly support *you* in living y*our* Purpose. When you write the rating down, keep in mind how they are currently living and what fear-based realities and thoughts they may have. You might want to take note of some of their fear-based realities so you can remember their states of consciousness.

I understand how doing that exercise might have made you feel somewhat uncomfortable, so I commend you for doing that.

Have you noticed any people from the list above that would support you with your Purpose-Driven Life? If so, fantastic! If not, no worries because you are about to open yourself to a whole new world before you.

Exercise: Inviting New Loved Ones Into Your Life

Preparation for Initiation

There are so many incredible people out there who are truly "living the life." They absolutely L-O-V-E their lives, and they would love to connect to people like you who want to live the kind of life they are living. They would be more than happy to be a guidepost for you to share and reflect with.

1. Take some time now to think about the kind of people you could meet who would be aligned with your Purpose. If your Purpose were to help people to be financially successful and to learn how to have fun with numbers and live incredibly free lives, then you would want to connect with a Financial Advisor. This Financial Advisor would be someone who absolutely adores numbers and loves and lives her Purpose fully. You can see she is a true success.

    First, think about your Divine Purpose Map and what amazing adventures you want to take in your life toward living your Purpose. Think about what types of people are living a Purpose similar to yours. Make a list in your journal of these types of people.

2. Next to the people you have listed, write down how you could meet them and have them be a part of your life. In some cases, it may be taking courses, joining meetup groups, being a part of a membership group where that person is the leader, or contacting the person directly and asking to have an interview with this person. There are private Facebook groups where like-minded people can gather and encourage each other on

their Vision and Mission. You could create positively driven accountability partners whom you meet up with weekly. Have fun with this, and let yourself be open-minded about how you can meet positively driven people.

◆

Great work! The next step is to start taking action on the above and find those groups you can join to be with positively driven, like-minded communities.

Initiation: Reuniting with Your Divine Soul Family

Guided by:
Goddess Daphne and Goddess Sophia

Close your eyes and take a couple of deep breaths. Feel yourself letting go of what you don't need right now.

Imagine yourself connected to Mother Earth. Just feel her warm embrace. Ask her to ground you through this experience.

Know that whatever your experience is, this is perfect for you and Divinely guided by your Inner Goddess.

It is a warm summer day.

Feel yourself standing by a beautiful beach.

You can feel the warm wind caressing your skin.

The sun is low on the horizon, and it is nearing sunset.

The sky is beginning to dance with colours.

You feel an incredible sense of peace envelop you as you look at the bright burnt orange of the sun.

Goddess Daphne walks along the sand and stands next to you.

She points to the beauty of the sun and smiles.

She then points to you and shares how beautiful you are, just like that sun.

HEAL & AWAKEN THE GODDESS WITHIN

She then invites you to stretch your arms outward and imagine your body is becoming a sail in the wind.

You can feel the wind at your back.

It is becoming so strong that you move your legs apart to stand better with the strong wind.

See the beauty, hear the wind, and feel the warmth.

This wind is here to guide you along your path.

Let your body be the sail in the wind now.

See your body become the sail, and the wind take you gracefully along your Purpose-Driven Path.

Feel the beauty of your sail taking you to majestic places.

Take some time to experience the places the wind is taking your sail to now.

You feel an incredible sense of safety, enthusiasm, and joy all at the same time.

You know you are on the precipice of significant change, and glory stands before you.

You see people all around you supporting you in living your wildest dreams.

Goddess Sophia steps in and shows you with her hands an array of incredible people who stand before you.

"These are your Soul Family," she says.

You are being initiated into your Soul Family once more so that you can fully invite them back into your life.

ALIGNING WITH POSITIVELY DRIVEN PEOPLE

Experience this initiation of togetherness and unification with your Soul Family now.

You may also notice guides, angels, goddesses, gods, and ascended masters joining you.

Take a moment to reflect and enjoy this joyous reunion with your Soul Family.

Embrace this moment and know that your Soul Family is here for you at all times.

Some may be living on Earth while others are on the other side.

Some of your Soul Family would like to speak to you now and share some messages that they feel would be helpful for you to know.

Take some time now to hear these beloved messages.

Take some time to thank your Soul Family for spending this precious time with you.

Goddess Daphne stands once more with you by the seaside.

She invites you to connect with her whenever you need guidance from the wind.

She is always here when you need to connect to your truest nature.

She is often by the beach, connected to nature.

Daphne says to you, "When you connect to nature, you are being shown your natural self."

"For it is you who are a part of nature.

"And I am here to remind you of that and to show you how to connect ever so deeply with beloved Gaia."

Take a moment to give thanks to beloved Goddess Daphne.

Goddess Sophia steps in, smiles at you, and points at your sacral area.

Goddess Sophia says to you, "It is here where you will birth all things.

"I am always here to assist you with your creations, as are your Beloved Soul Family.

"Aho."

Take a moment to give thanks to Beloved Goddess Sophia.

Whenever you are ready, you can slowly take a couple of deep breaths, bring your awareness to your eyes and slowly come back.

Reflections

You have received a beautiful initiation to reunite with your precious Soul Family, who are here to assist you in living your Holy Spirit's Divine Purpose.

Before getting up, take some time to be in this energy. You have had a very high-frequency initiation and activation. While you are in this energy, spend some time journaling your experience. As you journal, you will still be bathing in the warmth and love of Goddess Daphne and Goddess Sophia.

After journaling, spend some time letting this energy integrate into your system. You may feel the effects of it for up to 3 weeks. When you have received such high-frequency energy, it is essential to let your physical body slowly adapt to this shift.

Nurture yourself through this transformation by grounding yourself with healthy foods and walks in nature.

Take your time before moving on to the next chapter.

For now, enjoy spending time integrating and writing your experience in your journal.

ALIGNING WITH POSITIVELY DRIVEN PEOPLE

CHAPTER 14

HEALING FROM CORPORATE MENTALITY MINDSET

"You are an Image of the Divine Creator, Full of Unlimited Possibilities" - Goddess Athena

Rush, rush, rush. Do, do, do. Perform, perform, perform. This was the era of the Industrial Age, and it has crept into the Aquarian Age. The time is nigh to let the tides turn and wash over what no longer serves us.

Many do not realize how engrained people have become from the teachings of the Industrial Age. The leaders were often men, directing women on how to work efficiently in the factories. Women were taught how much freedom they could have by working and performing hard—the more dedicated, the better. The more pieces they could produce in a day, the higher their wage would be. Women came home feeling exhausted yet convinced that they were living a much better way of life. They felt content knowing they were putting more food on the table.

Men were convinced that working hard meant they had value to give this world. The harder they worked, the more valued they were by their bosses.

Having structure was paramount to achieving success. Over time, new systems were put in place to develop Continuous Improvement. More and more rules were made, making awareness of the connection to the Divine Mind clouded. Creating targeted goals in alignment with their Objectives became a standard talk. Even a SMART acronym was created not too long ago in coaching that made goal setting a "smart" thing to do.

Stress ensued. Anxiety, sickness, and depression started to hit in numbers. Finally, in the past decade, people taking sick leave became a common theme.

Mental Health Awareness became legislated in certain countries due to the increasing costs of people being on sick leave. Companies were ordered to discuss Mental Health and create procedures and policies to handle mental health issues.

Yet, through all of this, the elephant in the room was never discussed.

We have lost our connection to that which feeds our Soul and our intuition. Honouring ourselves is key to salvation.

Companies would be much more efficient if they brought forth qualities of the Holy Spirit into the Corporation. Giving a chance to honour people, listen to their needs and wisdom, and realize that they all bring unique gifts and talents would only enhance and assist with the healthy growth of the business.

The Corporation has turned humans into machines. I have heard firsthand from Managers saying, "Let's run them down until they almost break," "If they want to whine, they know where the door is. We don't need whiners," "They are faking their sickness, wanting just to be lazy," "This person is as dumb as rocks," "She just looks good," and many more atrocious statements over the years.

Those people lost one major thing: the connection to their Holy Spirit.

As a result of incessant brainwashing and control over the years, many women and men have become afraid of speaking up. They have come to fear losing their job. Panic and anxiety set in with even thinking about losing their job.

With that fear comes the inherent need to perform constantly. Rush, rush, rush. Do, do, do. Perform, perform, perform. Without performance, you will just become a number and be let go. And, without that job, there is no hope. The Corporation has made people feel like people only have value if they are acknowledged and given work by the Corporation. The more they rush, do, and perform, the more valued they are and the more freedom they have. Full stop.

This absurd teaching and brainwashing has been carried on for generations now and is carried on in our ancestral patterning. Our cells hold the makeup of these fear-based illusions.

Awareness must be made of how you operate in this world. So many people feel they need to perform and act to be a success. And, so, when living out your Purpose, your mind, more often than not, will automatically go into performance mode, believing that this is the ONLY way to success.

When going into performance mode, automatically thinking about what *should* be done next, you have lost your connection to the Divine Mind and your Holy Spirit. You see, it is here, where you lie in the bosom of your Holy Spirit, that you will receive all the nectar you need. The Divine Mind will show you all the guidance you need to fulfill your Divine Purpose on Earth.

To *fully* move forward, manifesting your Divine Purpose, you must let go of the illusory beliefs of the Corporate Mentality Mindset. That mindset will only create limitations that hold you back and force you into compliance with being chained down.

You deserve freedom, and I am taking a stand for humanity to receive this inherent freedom gifted to us all. We must take back our freedom and tell the Corporation, *"NO MORE!"*

Exercise: Becoming Aware of Corporate Mentality Mindset

Preparation for Initiation

You have taken incredible steps toward listening to the Divine Mind and your Holy Spirit by creating your Divine Purpose Map and laying out the next steps. Even though you have honoured this Divine Connection, it is still vital that you pay attention to the doer in you. The doer in you might revert to old patterns of rush, rush, rush, do, do, do, perform, perform, perform. The doer in you might go into the default mode of *thinking* to create your goals rather than connecting to the Divine Mind and listening to the Divine Guidance on setting goals.

You may have sometimes punished yourself for not performing the way you think you should. When you do this to yourself, allow yourself to take a moment, place your hands on your Sacred Heart and remind yourself that this came from social conditioning and Managers telling you how they *expect* you to behave.

It is time to heal from this bullshit. These conditionings have only held you back from living your ultimate desires and have taken away your freedom to choose how you create.

It is time to take back your freedom to choose how you want to live out your Divine Purpose and the freedom to manifest it in your own Divine Timing.

This also applies to you if you have never worked in the Corporate World, as you will have carried ancestral patterns in your cellular.

1. Take a moment to write in your journal thoughts over the past month that made you feel like you may not be performing enough or that you must complete x, y, and z first to achieve

your targeted goals. Pay attention if you had moments where you felt you had to follow a particular order to achieve things properly.

2. When you journal these thoughts, write what feelings come out through this process. Are you feeling saddened or irritated, scared or alone, etc.?

3. Have you noticed moments where you stray from living in the Circle (receiving guidance from the Divine Mind in *nonsequential* order) vs living linearly (receiving direction from the Limited Mind in *sequential* order)?

4. Lastly, write down the Divine Truth next to these limited thoughts. Remind yourself how powerful you are and how you are an Image of the Divine Creator, full of unlimited possibilities.

◆

You have taken a moment to respect yourself. This is something the Corporate World has stopped humanity from doing. Congratulations. You just took back your freedom to be and honoured your birthright.

Initiation: Taking Back Your Freedom

Guided by:
Elephant Spirit and Goddess Athena

Close your eyes and take a couple of deep breaths. Feel yourself letting go of what you don't need right now.

Imagine yourself connected to Mother Earth. Just feel her warm embrace. Ask her to ground you through this experience.

Know that whatever your experience is, this is perfect for you and Divinely guided by your Inner Goddess.

Feel Elephant Spirit running majestically through the field and gracefully coming towards you.

She slows down and stands beautifully before you.

You hear her breathing and sense her breath is welcoming you to her kingdom.

Take a moment to feel her presence.

Elephant Spirit lifts her trunk and gently places it on your head.

You can feel deep love and acknowledgement fill you.

You feel ever so profoundly touched by her presence.

As she continues holding her trunk over your crown, a necklace slides down from the top of her trunk over your head and onto your neck.

A colourful array of gemstones circle your neck.

HEALING FROM CORPORATE MENTALITY MINDSET

They are the perfect colours, designed especially for you.

"You are returning to Wholeness," Elephant Spirit says.

"These gemstones are to assist you in bringing back all aspects of yourself into this world.

"I empower you to take back all of you.

"You are now free."

Elephant Spirit lifts her trunk off your head and takes a few steps backwards.

She then bows down to you, honouring your Return to Wholeness.

As Elephant Spirit bows down to you, she initiates you into your Return to Wholeness.

Take a moment to experience this initiation.

As you return from your initiation, you look up at Elephant Spirit and notice Goddess Athena sitting on top of her.

"Rise," she says.

Elephant Spirit Rises.

As Elephant Spirit rises, you feel your energetic body rising to greater heights.

You feel yourself lighter and freer.

Goddess Athena reminds you of your incredible Divine Strength and Freedom.

She holds her staff and raises it toward the sky.

"Be the blazing torch unto this world," she says.

HEAL & AWAKEN THE GODDESS WITHIN

"Let yourself shine amongst the many.

"Take charge of the majestic strength within you.

"Know of your mighty Divine Intelligence.

"Keep steadfast in alignment with your Divine Guidance.

"It is here where you hold your Freedom steady.

"It is here where you are Whole."

Take a moment to feel this almighty strength and wisdom of Goddess Athena and Elephant Spirit.

Goddess Athena says, "I am here, eternally by your side. Call on me whenever you wish to cast away all doubt and empower yourself back to the restoration of your freedom."

"Make it so. Amen"

Take a moment to feel freedom being restored in your entire being.

Feel strength and wisdom being renewed.

You are one with freedom and control of your Divine Purpose.

Take a moment to give thanks to Elephant Spirit and Goddess Athena.

Whenever you are ready, you can slowly take a couple of deep breaths, bring your awareness to your eyes and slowly come back.

Reflections

You have received a very sacred blessing and initiation from Elephant Spirit and Goddess Athena. You are truly blessed that Elephant Spirit has come to initiate you into her kingdom.

Before getting up, take some time to be in this energy. You have had a very high-frequency initiation. While you are in this energy, spend some time journaling your experience. As you journal, you will still be bathing in the warmth and love of Elephant Spirit and Goddess Athena.

After journaling, spend some time letting this energy integrate into your system. You may feel the effects of it for up to 3 weeks. When you have received such high-frequency energy, it is essential to let your physical body slowly adapt to this shift.

Nurture yourself through this transformation by grounding yourself with healthy foods and walks in nature.

Take your time before moving on to the next chapter.

For now, enjoy spending time integrating and writing your experience in your journal.

HEAL & AWAKEN THE GODDESS WITHIN

HEALING FROM CORPORATE MENTALITY MINDSET

HEAL & AWAKEN THE GODDESS WITHIN

CHAPTER 15

EMBRACING MONEY

"Connect with the Brilliance of Your Inner Sacred Moon" - Mother Moon Spirit

You may have heard the old adage that Money is Energy, but it is so much more than that. To fully appreciate money, you must first remember to honour yourself. Ancient Greek teachings of the Moon show us specific techniques we can apply to ourselves to recognize and value our needs.

There is a significant correlation between the moon and money. The Moon has an impact on the waters of Beloved Gaia. The Moon will cause an ebb and flow of the waters, also known as tides. The high tide brings forth rushing, abundant waters and the low tide influences the waters' receding. This ebb and flow is a natural cycle of life. And, so, too, are you.

You may be wondering how this ebb and flow is related to the discussion of money. With tides, we have no control over how the Moon influences these tides. We have learned to honour each tide, for if we go against the tide, destruction ensues.

You may have moments of low and high tides in your life. These tides are divinely timed in the same way the Moon divinely times high and low tides. Instead of fighting low tides, helping to understand the significance of these low tides will aid you in using them to your optimum benefit.

Low tides are designed to enable you time to rest and create. If you consistently allow yourself to chase the high tide, your energy will eventually be depleted, like when playing non-stop in turbulent waters.

Many people chase after money for fear that they will never receive it. When you are sitting along the shoreline of a low tide, the high tide will slowly come in, caressing your legs. There is no need to run towards the receding tide, for it will return to you. During the low tide, you have an opportune time to sit by the shoreline, relax, meditate, and receive the dawn of new teachings that will take you to new heights with your Divine Purpose.

To receive money, allow yourself to connect inwards during the ebb stages. Connect with the Feminine Receiver of your Inner Goddess. During this stage, you may connect with Divine Teachings that will show you the next steps to take to receive the flow of the high tide with Grace.

◆

Exercise: Respecting the Tides of Your Sacred Moon

Preparation for Initiation

We all have Sacred Tides within us that result in ebbs and flows or moments of action and lulls. Healing and Awakening the Goddess Within asks us to honour the balance of the Divine Feminine and Divine Masculine within each of us. For years, we have mastered the skills of the Divine Masculine and have, more often than not, suppressed the Divine Feminine within us. When we honour our Sacred Moon Within, we can honour the high and low tides she influences.

1. Take a moment now to reflect on your past month. How often have you found yourself in the Active vs Reflective and Creative modes? Make a list in your journal of how your past month was concerning moving toward living out your Divine Purpose. Pay attention to the behaviours you have had. Did you find yourself very busy most of the time, consistently in Active Mode? When you were in low tide, were you honouring the Divine Feminine, allowing yourself to receive Divine Gifts? Sometimes, when we are in the low tide, we may self-sabotage, be hard on ourselves and do things that do not serve our Higher Purpose. Did you allow yourself grace and honour the Creator Within You during these times?

2. Write down what percentage of your time was spent in high tides vs low tides. How often did you honour the low tides? How often did you respect the high tides?

3. What can you do in the future to honour both tides so that you can be in balance with the Receiver and Creator during low tides and the Active person during high tides?

◆

When you honour the Divine Feminine, Masculine, and Sacred Moon within you, you can utilize the Great Power in the Universe to your considerable advantage.

Living in Sacred Balance of the Tides allows you to harness the energy of Money to its fullest capacity.

I honour you for honouring yourself.

Exercise: How You See Your Reflection

Preparation for Initiation

In Ancient Greek times, money was honoured and considered sacred. Money was to be respected in the same way the Moon and tides were respected. Money was a reflection of your Divine offerings. When looking in the water of a lake at nighttime, you see the beautiful reflection of Mother Moon. When the world looks at the waters before you, they will see your beautiful Moon and offerings shimmering in the water.

For others to see your magical gifts, your resonance must be equivalent to that which you want to be seen as. This means that you must feel the beauty and power of your magical gifts so that others can see the same within you.

What does your Moon look like as it reflects in the water in the night sky? Do you see the beautiful Moon shimmering in the water and reflecting its beauty back at you?

1. Take a moment to consider all the offerings you are about to bring into the world from your Divine Purpose Mapping exercise.

2. Write in your journal how you see yourself with what you can bring into the world for others. Do you see yourself as beautifully as you see the beauty of the Moon reflecting in the water on a night sky? Do you feel your Power and Greatness? Do you know this Greatness you hold? How are you, honestly, seeing yourself? Do you shimmer your brilliance for the world to see?

Be frank with yourself. It is essential to be honest so that you can become fully aware of your resonance and what you are reflecting out into the waters.

3. Write down what reflection people will be able to see in the water because of what you are emitting.

4. On a scale of 1 to 10, rate how strongly you radiate your incredible brilliance and the power of your Purpose and offerings.

5. Write down on a scale of 1 to 10 how strongly you believe you can make a significant change in this world with your Divine Offerings.

6. Write down what steps you can take to further align with *knowing* that you have Incredible Offerings to share with this world and that the world needs you. What do you need to do to reflect the Brilliance of your Sacred Moon?

Congratulations on taking a moment to be truly honest with yourself and seeing what it is you are reflecting out into the world. It is in the valuing of this reflection that you will invite money into your life. The more you honour *yourself*, the more others will see this valuable reflection.

Exercise: Embracing Money

Preparation for Initiation

Now that you know what steps need to be taken to shine your brilliance, we will discuss self-sabotage regarding money.

Over the years, there have been many beliefs and discussions that money is evil, money is selfish, money is greedy, and it is wrong to receive lots and lots of money. Those thoughts came from the Limited Mind and a fear-based reality.

Allowing yourself to receive an abundance of money reflects your self-love and love for others. When you receive lots of money, you will benefit in many ways. You will have time freedom, enabling you to experience more time to express yourself joyously. When you have an overflow of abundance, you can help others through philanthropy. Divine ideas would come streaming through with how you can help the world in ways you would never have been able to if you did not have the money.

Money enables you to hire a team of people whom you can also assist with living out their Divine Purpose. You can help them have the freedom to live the kind of life they desire, without having to push themselves, doing something they don't love.

Oprah is a living example of all the great things she has been able to do because of money.

You are not smaller than Oprah. You are just as Powerful. Only self-sabotage gets in the way of believing that you deserve an abundance of money.

1. Take a moment to write in your journal all the fantastic things you could do to make an incredible, positive impact in the world if you had much more money than you do today. Think BIG. Would you want to do anything philanthropic? How

would you like to help people or the environment? What would your life look like? Would you have more time freedom? What would be important to you?

2. How much money would you need to make annually to accomplish those incredible items you discussed in Step 1?

3. On a scale of 1 to 10, rate how much you believe you can receive the money you wrote in Step 2 to do all those things you listed in Step 1.

4. Write down what you need to do to shift perspective around your beliefs about money so you can receive this abundance.

You deserve to live a life of abundance so that you can fully live a joyous life and contribute to making this world a better place.

For too long, people have defaulted on punishing themselves for thinking about wanting more money. As a result, so many people have struggled in their lives. It is time that we change this limited mentality mindset.

Congratulations on taking steps to heal and grow beyond your wildest dreams.

Initiation: Honouring the Sacred Moon Within You

Guided by:
Mother Moon Spirit

Close your eyes and take a couple of deep breaths. Feel yourself letting go of what you don't need right now.

Imagine yourself connected to Mother Earth. Just feel her warm embrace. Ask her to ground you through this experience.

Know that whatever your experience is, this is perfect for you and Divinely guided by your Inner Goddess.

Feel the Divine Presence of Mother Moon Spirit descend upon you now.

"I AM here. Feel me," she says.

"Can you feel the Greatness that I AM?

"Let me be the Light that shines upon your altar.

"Let me shimmer in your lovely pool.

"It is here where you see the Greatness that I AM."

Take a moment and experience this beautiful reflection of Mother Moon Spirit in the water before you.

Let this Divine Reflection of Mother Moon Spirit fill you up.

Mother Moon Spirit places a Divine Coin in your hands.

EMBRACING MONEY

"Receive this Divine Coin as a reflection of your worth," Mother Moon Spirit says.

"You are Divinely Worthy, my dear, sweet Soul.

"Feel the abundance of coins shower over you now as you look up into the sky.

"May each coin represent all the tremendous Souls you are about to embrace in your life.

"These Souls are all coming to you because they know you can help them.

"Feel the gratitude of all these Souls shower upon you.

"Feel all these Souls waiting for you to come and help them."

A great big smile shines upon your face, for you feel so touched and honoured to assist with the transformation of so many lives.

Take a moment to feel the transformation of all those lives you will be touching.

Mother Moon Spirit now points to the waters before you.

She invites you to see the beautiful reflection that your Inner Moon emanates into these waters.

Mother Moon Spirit says, "You see how beautiful you are?"

You feel incredible healing taking place in your Sacred Heart as you look down at your luminescent reflection.

"There is a whole world before you, awaiting your embrace," she says.

Feel your body, mind, and Soul resonating with the Divine Truth of your Sacred Inner Moon.

You feel so honoured and treasured.

You have come home to the Divine Truth of the Sacred Moon within you.

Take a moment to receive Divine Teachings from your Sacred Moon.

"Divine Abundance flows through you now," says Mother Moon Spirit.

"The world awaits your precious gifts.

"Whenever you look at my reflection shimmering in the night, remember your Divine Brilliance.

"See our brilliance shimmering together as we send our gifts out into this world.

"I AM Mother Moon Spirit and am with you always."

Take a moment to give thanks to Mother Moon Spirit.

Whenever you are ready, you can slowly take a couple of deep breaths, bring your awareness to your eyes and slowly come back.

Reflections

You have received an initiation from Mother Moon Spirit to Heal and Awaken to the Abundance that exists within you and to honour the receiving of this Abundance you so deeply deserve. You are a Divine, precious Soul. You have been initiated into the Brilliance of your Inner Sacred Moon.

Before getting up, take some time to be in this energy. You have had a very high-frequency initiation. While you are in this energy, spend some time journaling your experience. As you journal, you will still be bathing in the warmth and love of Mother Moon Spirit.

After journaling, spend some time letting this energy integrate into your system. You may feel the effects of it for up to 3 weeks. When you have received such high-frequency energy, it is essential to let your physical body slowly adapt to this shift.

Nurture yourself through this transformation by grounding yourself with healthy foods and walks in nature.

Take your time before moving on to the next chapter.

For now, enjoy spending time integrating and writing your experience in your journal.

EMBRACING MONEY

HEAL & AWAKEN THE GODDESS WITHIN

CHAPTER 16

HONOURING YOUR MAGNIFICENCE

"It is in Your Knowing that Your Manifestations are Fully Realized" - Goddess Athena

You are a Brilliant Being, full of incredible Magnificence. You have come to the place in your journey where you have seen your extraordinary gifts and Divine Purpose. You have been asked to check in with yourself to become aware of your mindset regarding abundance and Sacred Money. You now have all the tools necessary to begin your creative process toward living your Divine Purpose.

One common theme that tends to creep up at this stage in your progress is the fear of being as Magnificent as you are fully capable of being. This is a feeling most people acquire due to the subconscious fear of being unsafe. You have dealt with most of this unconscious fear in earlier chapters where we addressed current-life trauma, past-life trauma, and ancestral trauma in your cellular.

Our minds, however, have been trained to think in a specific, repetitive way. We have been trained to believe in our current reality. In other words, we have been trained to believe in what we see rather than *knowing* the Power of the Divine and its Possibilities.

As a result, we play small because we have a hard time believing that such Greatness is possible. Since we don't see it occurring in our lives now, we tell ourselves that such Greatness is merely a fantasy and only possible for the privileged or the elite.

We must address this part of ourselves and move towards a newly trained mindset.

You deserve to live a remarkable life. To live this glorious purposeful life, honouring your Divine Magnificence is paramount. You must *know* this Magnificence is here to experience in your everyday life. Until you *know* this Magnificence exists, you cannot receive it.

This thought can be scary because most people around you walk in this life playing small. They have been taught to believe that what is out there is the only real thing. Should you share your "scary" dreams with the world, most people will chastise you and tell you that your ambitions are ludicrous.

I'm here to tell you that the opposite is true. It is ludicrous NOT to see your Divine Magnificence and NOT to believe you can manifest this Greatness in the here and now. Your Holy Spirit does not want you to experience this power only in energetic form. Your Holy Spirit wants you to live out your Brilliance in this world.

So, how do you honour your Magnificence when the mind is thinking small? Practice becoming aware of your thoughts and shift your focus toward your desired *outcome*. *Feel* the *result* of your Divine Purpose *fully manifested*. *Feel* this in your Divine Temple. Imagine this incredible Magnificence you have to share in this world *fully realized*. See all the people you will touch positively impacted by your Brilliant Manifestations. *Feel* the joy in your body and *know* this outcome to be true. *Know* that the Divine responds to your calling. The most important part is to understand that the Divine responds to your *knowing* that your greatest desires are being fully manifested. In essence, the Divine is a mirror of you, for you are one with the Divine. If you think small, all you will get is small. The Divine can only respond to what you *know* to be true.

You do not need to worry about the *how*. The *how* is given to you when the Divine responds to your radiating the *knowing* that your Divine Purpose is being fully manifested. This *knowing* must occur *before* it exists in your outside reality. This is Divine Law.

The Power of your Magnificence exists within you, NOT outside of you.

♦

Exercise: Becoming Aware of How Small You are Playing

Preparation for Initiation & Activation

To manifest your Magnificence, it is essential to become aware of the thoughts occurring in your head when you contemplate living your Divine Purpose.

1. Take a moment to write in your journal your self-limiting beliefs regarding the plans you would like to make toward living out your Divine Purpose. Pay attention to what you tell yourself. For example, you may say to yourself:

    - I don't have enough time;
    - It will take a very long time to manifest;
    - It will cost too much money;
    - I can't make a living doing this;
    - That thought is too powerful;
    - I'm not that powerful;
    - I don't think I can be that powerful;
    - Those dreams are too big;

- Those dreams are impossible to achieve; or
- Only certain people can achieve a goal like that.

2. Write down what you could be thinking instead of these self-limiting beliefs.

◆

What you have done is paramount to ensuring you manifest your Divine Purpose. I honour you for taking those steps toward being even more aware of your thoughts and what may be holding you back from experiencing your Divine Greatness here on Beloved Gaia.

◆

Exercise: Creating Your Reality

Preparation for Initiation & Activation

1. Take some time now to be creative and write in detail the experiences you would have in life with your Divine Purpose fully manifested. When writing your experiences, consider these:
    - Describe what your life would look like.
    - Go into detail about your feelings.
    - Describe in detail the Magnificence you will have manifested.
    - Describe how the people you help will be impacted.
    - Describe in detail what your friends and family will be feeling.

    Allow yourself plenty of time to write. Let this experience be pages long. Keep writing in your journal until you feel these words strongly and you feel an inner *knowing* that your Divine Purpose Map will be fully manifested.

This is a powerful exercise you can do to honour your Magnificence and allow the Universe to do its work to make it manifest fully.

It is crucial to take some time every day, preferably 2 to 4 times a day and feel these manifestations in your body. Honour yourself some time to go through the visualization you wrote and feel the excitement of these manifestations in your body. Doing this daily allows the Divine to respond with likeness. The *how* will be shown to you in countless ways as a result.

Initiation & Activation: Honouring Your Magnificence

Guided by:
Goddess Athena

Close your eyes and take a couple of deep breaths. Feel yourself letting go of what you don't need right now.

Imagine yourself connected to Mother Earth. Just feel her warm embrace. Ask her to ground you through this experience.

Know that whatever your experience is, this is perfect for you and Divinely guided by your Inner Goddess.

Feel the bright yellow Aura of Goddess Athena stepping in.

"You are Brilliant like the Sun," Goddess Athena says.

"Feel your brightness illumine from the inside out.

"Discover this brightness as you see your Brilliance.

"Let your Brilliance shine even greater than the Sun.

"Feel joy emanate from your Being.

"You are luminescent and radiate ever so brightly.

"I honour this treasure house within you.

"Feel your Magnificence activating within you now."

Take some time now to feel this activation from Goddess Athena.

Goddess Athena says, "You are Brilliant down to your very core.

"Understand this. It is through your understanding that you will come to know this.

"It is in this inner knowing that all gifts are revealed.

"It is in this inner knowing where your manifestations are fully realized."

Take some time now to feel and visualize your Beloved Purpose being Manifested.

Goddess Athena says, "I AM here with you always, cheering you on, for you are Divine Greatness, and the time has come for the world to see your Magnificence manifested in the here and now.

"I thank you for knowing your Divine Purpose as fully manifested in all its Magnificence.

"Let this inner knowing fully vibrate in your entire body and Aura.

"May this consecration be a pillar to light you up with your manifestations forever more.

"And, so it is.

"I remain forever yours."

Take a moment to give thanks to Goddess Athena.

Whenever you are ready, you can slowly take a couple of deep breaths, bring your awareness to your eyes and slowly come back.

Reflections

You have received an initiation and activation from Goddess Athena into the Magnificence of your Divine Power.

Before getting up, take some time to be in this energy. You have had a very high-frequency initiation and activation. While you are in this energy, spend some time journaling your experience. As you journal, you will still be bathing in the warmth and love of Goddess Athena.

After journaling, spend some time letting this energy integrate into your system. You may feel the effects of it for up to 3 weeks. When you have received such high-frequency energy, it is essential to let your physical body slowly adapt to this shift.

Nurture yourself through this transformation by grounding yourself with healthy foods and walks in nature.

Take your time before moving on to the next chapter.

For now, enjoy spending time integrating and writing your experience in your journal.

HONOURING YOUR MAGNIFICENCE

CHAPTER 17

EMBRACING YOUR INNER SAVIOUR

*"Trust that the Divine is Here to Serve You" -
Beloved Quan Yin*

Who is this Internal Saviour, anyway? Plain and simple—it is YOU. How does it feel to know that YOU will take yourself to great heights?

We are so used to climbing mountains with a partner to keep us safe that when it comes to daily living, our default can often be the need to have a Saviour take all our struggles away and make everything e-a-s-y for us.

How willing are you to get out of your comfort zone to live a life of your calling?

Are you comfortable with the status quo?

You have come to these teachings for a Great reason. This reason is to Heal and Awaken the Goddess Within so that you may Awaken to your Purpose and L-I-V-E your Divine Calling.

You have had incredible Healing during our journey together. You have cleared so much fear, anxiety, and trauma from this life, past lives, and ancestral lives, and I commend you for that!

You have had a great Awakening during our journey together. You have reunited with your Holy Spirit. You have become aware of your Passions and Strengths. You made great strides in Mapping out your Divine Purpose.

You discovered what actions to take that would align you with living your Divine Purpose. You learned that the Divine Mind is the one who gives you Divine Directions so that you can achieve your accomplishments with greater ease.

When people reach this point, some old *subconscious* patterns kick in of wanting to be saved. Many people have had tough lives. As a result, many have needed and wanted help with those challenging tasks that life has dealt them.

Here's the thing: to make your life easier, you Get to Allow yourself to take the necessary steps that you have been guided to take by the Divine Mind toward Living your Divine Purpose.

When you *Allow* yourself to start your journey on your path of living your Divine Purpose, you give yourself an opportunity to live a life you had never before been able to even dream of.

This is where trust comes into play. Due to all the challenges, fears, and traumas we have faced, it has become unnatural to trust in the Divine. When the Divine cannot be trusted, people turn to an external Saviour to comfort them and help make life e-a-s-y. Taking that so-called easy path makes you feel unfulfilled because your Soul knows it is not living your Holy Spirit's Purpose. The sense of unfulfillment is your Soul speaking to you, telling you how your path is impacting you.

Most of society has learned how to avoid things. Avoidance leads to safety. It also leads to experiencing great struggles and to playing small. When we avoid, we resist the Flow of the Divine. You are not allowing the Divine Mind to guide you when you play small.

Are you able to trust that the Divine is here to *serve* you? The nature of the Divine is to provide you with e-a-s-e. Are you ready to welcome this and step into your Greatest Power to live your Divine Purpose?

Exercise: Inviting Trust Back Into Your Life

Preparation for Initiation & Activation

This exercise is more about inner reflection. Take a moment to think about your Divine Purpose Map and the Actions listed to live your Purpose. As you do this, think about your current life.

1. On a scale of 1 to 10, write in your journal where you are now regarding taking the actions from your Action list toward living your Divine Purpose.

2. Next, write down on a scale of 1 to 10 how much you wish someone else could take care of the Actions for you so that you can live your Purpose now.

3. Write down on a scale of 1 to 10 how excited you are about taking action so you can live your Divine Calling.

4. Write down on a scale of 1 to 10 how much you trust you can fully live your Purpose according to your Divine Purpose Map.

5. Lastly, write down what you need to do to bridge the gap from needing an External Saviour to take care of things for you to empowering yourself with the Saviour within you and trusting that you can manifest living your Purpose with joy.

Honouring yourself and checking in to do some self-reflection is paramount to understanding where we are at and what we may be avoiding. We must remember that we have developed patterns for centuries (not just from this life) that have kept us feeling safe.

Although you have transmuted past-life trauma and ancestral trauma earlier during these teachings, old patterns can creep up because we have been used to living this way. It is essential to be aware of these old patterns that come up so that we can realize what needs to be shifted to allow Greatness to come into our lives.

Initiation & Activation: Embracing Your Inner Saviour

Guided by:

Quan Yin and Archangel Raphael

Close your eyes and take a couple of deep breaths. Feel yourself letting go of what you don't need right now.

Imagine yourself connected to Mother Earth. Just feel her warm embrace. Ask her to ground you through this experience.

Know that whatever your experience is, this is perfect for you and Divinely guided by your Inner Goddess.

Feel the sweet, compassionate presence of Beloved Quan Yin and the beautiful healing energy of Archangel Raphael enter your field now.

Your Aura fills with beautiful emerald green from Quan Yin and yellowish green from Archangel Raphael.

Take some time to feel their energy clearing your Aura.

"You are a Divine Presence," they both say to you.

"Know that this Divine Presence is one with you.

"We invite you to welcome Trust back into your life fully and completely in this very moment."

Quan Yin and Archangel Raphael invite you to see yourself scooping up your arms and bathing yourself with their healing auras.

HEAL & AWAKEN THE GODDESS WITHIN

Feel your body bathing in this healing energy.

Allow yourself to open your Sacred Heart.

Quan Yin and Archangel Raphael are activating your Sacred Heart now so that you are once again led by trust.

Take some time now to experience this activation.

See yourself reuniting with the Saviour Within You now.

See your Holy Spirit climbing down your Golden Rope to meet and talk to you now.

Listen to the Wise Teachings your Holy Spirit has to say to you regarding embracing your internal Saviour and naturally inviting Trust fully into your life.

Take a moment to thank your Holy Spirit for always being here with you.

Beloved Quan Yin and Archangel Raphael come to you once more and gift you a token of remembrance for activating your Sacred Heart to embrace trust.

Quan Yin and Archangel Raphael thank you for being here and invite you to call upon them whenever you need a warm embrace.

They love you dearly.

Take a moment to give thanks to Beloved Quan Yin and Archangel Raphael.

Whenever you are ready, you can slowly take a couple of deep breaths, bring your awareness to your eyes and slowly come back.

Reflections

You have received an initiation and activation from Beloved Quan Yin and Archangel Raphael so that Trust entirely leads you.

Before getting up, take some time to be in this energy. You have had a very high-frequency initiation and activation. While you are in this energy, spend some time journaling your experience. As you journal, you will still be bathing in the warmth and love of Quan Yin and Archangel Raphael.

After journaling, spend some time letting this energy integrate into your system. You may feel the effects of it for up to 3 weeks. When you have received such high-frequency energy, it is essential to let your physical body slowly adapt to this shift.

Nurture yourself through this transformation by grounding yourself with healthy foods and walks in nature.

Take your time before moving on to the next chapter.

For now, enjoy spending time integrating and writing your experience in your journal.

HEAL & AWAKEN THE GODDESS WITHIN

EMBRACING YOUR INNER SAVIOUR

CHAPTER 18

GOING DEEP

"Allowing Yourself to Go Deep Opens the Door to Immense Freedom" - Goddess Hecate

You have embraced your Magnificence, and I congratulate you on that! You have gone deep and cleared out memories from your cellular that came from your past lives, ancestral lives, and this life. With every trauma clearing, layers of clearing occur, depending upon what you are energetically and physically ready to have cleared. In other words, it would be impossible to remove everything all at once because that would be like having a lightning bolt strike you and you feeling okay afterwards. During your initiations and activations, massive, powerful energy is soaring through you to do its work to raise you and clear away what no longer serves you. The Divine knows how much your body can handle emotionally and physically. Thus, you will receive the degree of healing that your body and mind can take.

Goddess Hecate brings you additional healing to take the clearing to the next level. She says that many of you would not have been able to handle this level of healing until you spent time integrating the energies that have taken you to the point where you are today.

Now, it is time to go deep. It is time to allow the next level of deep healing to occur. "You are so ready for this," Goddess Hecate wants you to know.

Goddess Hecate explains that in ancient times, there were warriors who blasphemed the elite. These elite were those who were deeply connected to their intuition. They would roam the world knowing who they were and would help humanity in large numbers. They assisted in the Awakening of those lost in the underworld, freeing these individuals from their darkness. So many began walking freely as Awakened ones, fully connected to the Divine.

You were one of those intuitive people who lived during those times. During the darkening of this Age, you and many others experienced the worst possible nightmares. People were maimed, raped, tortured, and beaten, and many experienced sacrificial death. Some of these painful sacrifices were long and drawn out, so these intuitive people were forced to experience the most tortuous deaths possible.

You have come here to Heal and Awaken The Goddess Within to be completely healed of this past pain and entirely free to be the gifted Intuitive you are.

Most intuitive people are terrified of walking fully in their Divine Gift. This pain experienced during the Light Ages' dampening into the Dark Ages was unbearable. To this day, this memory has been anchored deeply in cellular memory.

Now that you have healed so many incredible layers of trauma from past lives, ancestral lives, and this life, your body is ready to release the deepest level of trauma. Releasing this deep-seated trauma requires inviting in specialized high-frequency energy that knows how to send love to this trauma and provide you with the necessary healing.

"You are so ready for this. You are so ready." Goddess Hecate says to you. She wants you to know that there is nothing to fear; instead, there is so much joy to gain in the discovery that you are entirely safe to express your Divine Intuitive Nature fully. She says, "You are ready to be this full expression, and now your body and mind are being prepared to unite with this natural part of you so that you can once more walk freely, sharing your Intuitive Gift without having to play small."

◆

Exercise: Going Deep

Preparation for Initiation

Allow yourself to go deep with this exercise to prepare for your initiation. The deeper you go, the more healing you will allow yourself during the initiation.

This exercise must be done in the dark, where you see no light inside your room. All lights must be turned off, and you must be alone. Curtains or blinds should be closed to not allow any outside night light inside the room.

Grab a recording device, such as your phone. You will record what comes to you during this exercise rather than write it down. If you do not have access to a recording device, you can take notes mentally; when you are done with the exercise, you can write down what you remember.

It is essential to stay in this state in complete darkness while doing the exercise.

Are you ready? Great! You are about to take some time now in complete darkness where there are no distracting noises. If there are noises, put some earplugs in or wait until there are no noises surrounding you. You will need to feel as though you are entirely alone. Take the following steps while you are in the darkness:

1. If you are recording from your phone, you may need to put your phone in airplane mode so that the recording doesn't stop if you suddenly get a message. This has happened to me more than once.

2. Turn the face of your phone down onto the floor so that you don't see any light coming from your phone.

3. Sit upright, and do not put any blanket on you. Just allow yourself to be warm enough with the clothes you are wearing.

4. Take some deep breaths and feel yourself centring into your being.

5. Imagine yourself living out your Divine Purpose Map 1000%, completely and fully, whereby you are 1000% fully expressive NOW and liberated to do everything at this moment to live out your Purpose.

6. Now, place your mind and feelings deep into the cellular structure. Invite the fears that are hidden deep down in your cells to show you what those fears are.

7. Voice record what fears arise regarding being 1000% fully expressive NOW and living out your Purpose NOW.

8. Allow your mind and emotions to go deeper into your cells to experience more awareness of these fears.

9. Keep voice recording each fear that comes to your awareness.

10. Allow yourself to get deep into fears that are primal in nature. Some past hidden fears that will rise to the surface during this exercise originated from when your freedom of expression was suppressed in another life. Ask your body what would happen if the subconscious absolute worst-case scenario occurred.

11. Keep going until you no longer have any new fears coming to the surface. Try and allow at least eight fears to come into your awareness during this process.

12. When you feel complete, come back and write all those fears down.

13. Immediately afterward, move on to the subsequent initiation, whereby Goddess Hecate will come to assist you with releasing all these anchored fears.

◆

You have done massive work, and it takes immense courage to do what you just did. Taking time to deeply feel and sense what deep-seated fears exist in your body is a tremendous accomplishment.

Please go ahead now and do the initiation with Goddess Hecate, who will assist you with transmuting these fears that have been stored in your body for far too long. Before you start the initiation, take a moment to recall the fears you listed, as you will be addressing these fears in the initiation. During the initiation, allow yourself to go back into complete darkness and make sure there is no noise around you. Wear some earplugs if you need to keep sounds out.

Initiation: Going Deep

Guided by:
Goddess Hecate

Close your eyes and take a couple of deep breaths. Feel yourself letting go of what you don't need right now.

Imagine yourself connected to Mother Earth. Just feel her warm embrace. Ask her to ground you through this experience.

Know that whatever your experience is, this is perfect for you and Divinely guided by your Inner Goddess.

Goddess Hecate steps in.

Feel the powerful presence of Goddess Hecate.

As you do so, you can feel powerful energy filling your Aura.

Notice this powerful energy filling up with a very dark purple. The purple is so dark; it is almost black.

Feel your entire room filled with Goddess Hecate's dark purple Aura.

As Goddess Hecate stands before you, she holds her hands toward you and tells you that you are about to slowly release to her, one by one, each fear you have discovered lying within you. She asks that you do so only upon her command.

"Release to me fear number one now," she says.

GOING DEEP

See yourself releasing fear number one from your body and Aura, and you see her receiving this fear with her hands.

Watch her as she transmutes fear number one.

Goddess Hecate says, "Be a witness to this fear being transmuted once and for all."

Experience your body feeling lighter.

"Release to me fear number two now," she says.

See yourself releasing fear number two from your body and Aura, and you see her receiving this fear with her hands.

Watch her as she transmutes fear number two.

Goddess Hecate says, "Be a witness to this fear being transmuted once and for all."

Experience your body feeling even lighter.

"Release to me fear number three now," she says.

See yourself releasing fear number three from your body and Aura, and you see her receiving this fear with her hands.

Watch her as she transmutes fear number three.

Goddess Hecate says, "Be a witness to this fear being transmuted once and for all."

Experience your body feeling even lighter.

"Release to me fear number four now," she says.

See yourself releasing fear number four from your body and Aura, and you see her receiving this fear with her hands.

HEAL & AWAKEN THE GODDESS WITHIN

Watch her as she transmutes fear number four.

Goddess Hecate says, "Be a witness to this fear being transmuted once and for all."

Experience your body feeling even lighter.

"Release to me fear number five now," she says.

See yourself releasing fear number five from your body and Aura, and you see her receiving this fear with her hands.

Watch her as she transmutes fear number five.

Goddess Hecate says, "Be a witness to this fear being transmuted once and for all."

Experience your body feeling even lighter.

"Release to me fear number six now," she says.

See yourself releasing fear number six from your body and Aura, and you see her receiving this fear with her hands.

Watch her as she transmutes fear number six.

Goddess Hecate says, "Be a witness to this fear being transmuted once and for all."

Experience your body feeling even lighter.

"Release to me fear number seven now," she says.

See yourself releasing fear number seven from your body and Aura, and you see her receiving this fear with her hands.

Watch her as she transmutes fear number seven.

GOING DEEP

Goddess Hecate says, "Be a witness to this fear being transmuted once and for all."

Experience your body feeling even lighter.

"Release to me fear number eight now," she says.

See yourself releasing fear number eight from your body and Aura, and you see her receiving this fear with her hands.

Watch her as she transmutes fear number eight.

Goddess Hecate says, "Be a witness to this fear being transmuted once and for all."

Experience your body feeling even lighter.

"Release to me anything you have forgotten to release now," she says.

See yourself releasing these fears from your body and Aura, and you see her receiving these fears with her hands.

Watch her as she transmutes these fears.

Goddess Hecate says, "Be a witness to these fears being transmuted once and for all."

Experience your body feeling even lighter.

"You have done great work," she says.

"You have just liberated yourself into your greatest possible freedom to make choices towards your greatest desires.

"You are free to fully and safely express yourself, knowing that your full expression will liberate others.

"This is what you deserve, and this is what they deserve.

"Go now and be the Initiate and Awaken Humanity.

"This is your calling and why you came here.

"I AM by your side, assisting you with expressing your intuitive gifts.

"Now is the time to create a new world and undo past wrongs

"Thank you for choosing to heal and transform the world."

Take a moment to give thanks to Goddess Hecate.

Whenever you are ready, you can slowly take a couple of deep breaths, bring your awareness to your eyes and slowly come back.

Reflections

You have received profound healing and an initiation from Goddess Hecate.

Before getting up, take some time to be in this energy. You have had a very high-frequency initiation. While you are in this energy, spend some time journaling your experience. As you journal, you will still be experiencing the incredible healing power of Goddess Hecate.

After journaling, spend some time letting this energy integrate into your system. You may feel the effects of it for up to 3 weeks. When you have received such high-frequency energy, it is essential to let your physical body slowly adapt to this shift.

Nurture yourself through this transformation by grounding yourself with healthy foods and walks in nature.

Take your time before moving on to the next chapter.

For now, enjoy spending time integrating and writing your experience in your journal.

GOING DEEP

HEAL & AWAKEN THE GODDESS WITHIN

CHAPTER 19

ALIGNING WITH YOUR DIVINE PURPOSE

"Steer Yourself in the Direction of Your Divine Purpose" - Lord Lanto

Do you align with your Divine Purpose before you get out of bed? Do you check in with yourself regularly throughout the day regarding how you are living in alignment with your Divine Purpose? How oriented are you toward living your Holy Spirit's calling?

These are all questions to ponder so that you remember clearly why you came here.

We are all human, and until old patterns are completely shifted, most people will repeat old ways of behaving and forget what is most important to them. For you to continually be oriented towards your Holy Spirit's calling, you will need a guidepost to keep you oriented in this direction.

This guidepost is your Personal or Business Vision and Mission Statements. Your Vision Statement represents your impact on this world when living your Divine Purpose. Your Mission Statement describes what you will do to make that impact.

If you plan on having a business, it is vital that you market to people who will need the kind of help that is in alignment with your Vision and Mission Statements. You will also want to align all your services and products with your Vision and Mission Statements. In other words, your services and products should provide your customers with an end result that is directly aligned with the impact you will make for them based on your ultimate Mission and Vision. This means that your messaging for your products and services should be aligned with your Mission and Vision. With this approach, your customers will be clear about how you can help them. This will make you uniquely stand out with your Individualized Purpose.

Once you have created these Vision and Mission Statements, I highly recommend you connect with them daily to feel their power. Let them be your guidepost on how you live out your life daily. Your Vision and Mission will assist you in steering consistently in the direction of your Holy Spirit's greatest desires.

◆

Exercise: Vision Statement

Preparation for Initiation & Activation

It is time to put down in words what your ultimate Vision is for humanity. This Vision is based on the impact you will make when living your Divine Purpose.

When writing your Vision Statement, you can write out a short sentence or even a couple of words as a statement. When creating a Vision Statement, you want to answer the question: What ultimate impact are you making in the world by living your Divine Purpose?

This question can scare some people, as they are uncomfortable with including themselves as making a significant impact in the world. I'm here to tell you that you DO significantly impact the world. Now is the time to honour the significance you make in the world. When you create your Vision Statement, allow yourself the honour of *knowing* you do and will significantly impact the world.

ALIGNING WITH YOUR DIVINE PURPOSE

When you write your Vision Statement, dream big and let yourself feel like a kid again.

A Vision Statement should feel scary because it invites you to play BIG. It is asking you to listen to your Holy Spirit and let your Holy Spirit be the guide in your life. It invites you to DO what your Holy Spirit asks you to do. That is huge!

1. Go back to your Divine Purpose Map, where you have listed your Divine Strengths, Purpose, and what you can do to live your Divine Purpose.

2. Take some time to write in your journal different Vision Statements until you feel you have nailed the perfect Vision Statement. Remember, this Vision Statement represents the impact that will be made in the world from you living your Divine Purpose.

   Examples of Vision Statements are:
   - Happy Women
   - A World filled with Happy Women
   - A World full of Clean Air
   - Pets Running Around with Smiles on their Faces
   - A World filled with Happy Pets

Great work! You have just narrowed down in a short sentence how you will impact the world in a HUGE way. Congratulations!

Exercise: Mission Statement

Preparation for Initiation & Activation

Now that you have your Vision Statement written, you will write out what you will do to accomplish your Vision. This is your Mission Statement. This ultimately represents what you plan to do to help achieve this incredible Vision of yours.

Sometimes, people get caught up in too many details when they write Mission Statements. For example, if it is a business Mission Statement, they may write out details of the modalities they use in their business, such as coaching, reiki, hypnotherapy, etc. These tools help you with your Mission; however, you do not need to mention these specific tools. It may help to list them in some cases, but it is unnecessary in most cases.

Your Mission Statement guides you to stay oriented toward your vision to stay on track.

Your Mission Statement also helps others to understand whether you can be of help to them.

Your Mission Statement summarizes your Divine Purpose Map. Take a look at your Divine Purpose Map and see how you can best describe what you will do to achieve your Vision.

1. Take time to write in your journal various Mission Statements until you feel you have nailed the perfect Mission Statement.

    Examples of Mission Statements are:

    - I help women discover inner happiness so that they can experience daily joy.
    - I help women feel confident looking at numbers, enabling them to clear their debt and create a life of abundance.

ALIGNING WITH YOUR DIVINE PURPOSE

- ❖ I teach pet owners how to communicate with their pets so that their pets can live happier lives.
- ❖ I awaken humanity to their inner freedom.

Outstanding effort! I know what it takes to write a Vision and Mission Statement, and I know it may involve extra time with writing and rewriting for many people. Writing these Statements should make you feel as though you just wrote what truly represents your Divine Purpose. If you don't feel complete, spend time writing new Vision and Mission Statements until you get that warm and fuzzy feeling inside of you.

Initiation & Activation: Holy of Holies

Guided by:
Lord Lanto and Mary Magdalene

Close your eyes and take a couple of deep breaths. Feel yourself letting go of what you don't need right now.

Imagine yourself connected to Mother Earth. Just feel her warm embrace. Ask her to ground you through this experience.

Know that whatever your experience is, this is perfect for you and Divinely guided by your Inner Goddess.

Feel the Presence of Lord Lanto streaming through your Aura.

Lord Lanto immediately brings forth his mantle of yellowish gold down through your spine.

Feel this energy extending above and below into the Universe.

He now sends a ray of yellow light across your Sacred Heart.

Feel this ray emanating from your Sacred Heart above and below and side to side into the Universe.

Mary Magdalene ignites your Sacred Heart with passionate pink energy.

Feel this pink and yellow energy stemming from your Sacred Heart and extending outwards, above and below, and side to side.

"Remember who you are," Mary Magdalene says.

"Wake up each morning remembering who you are

ALIGNING WITH YOUR DIVINE PURPOSE

"THIS is your calling."

Lord Lanto and Mary Magdalene point at your Sacred Heart and invite you to now connect with your Holy Spirit.

You feel a beam of energy streaming to your Holy Spirit.

Your Holy Spirit climbs down the golden rope to meet you once more.

Your Holy Spirit speaks to you now and shares a message on how to align with your Holy Spirit every day.

Take a moment to hear your Holy Spirit's message.

Mary Magdalene invites you to follow her to a Sacred Chamber.

She sits down and invites you to sit with her, facing her.

"Look into my eyes," she says.

Mary Magdalene will initiate you now into the Holy of Holies as a High Priestess/Priest/Priestex and activate your Sacred Heart, Soul, and mind in alignment with this sacred energy.

Spend some time now experiencing this sacred initiation and activation.

"It is here where you may experience your Sacred Torch. It is here where you may touch hands with the Almighty," Mary says.

"It is here where you are united with the Great Presence I AM THAT I AM."

Immerse yourself in this Divine Presence within the Holy of Holies now.

"Remember who you are," Mary says to you.

Before Mary leaves, she invites you to return to this Sacred Chamber whenever you wish, and you may call upon her to activate your connection with the Holy of Holies.

Mary blesses you and leaves you to continue experiencing this Divine Connection in the Sacred Chamber for as long as you need.

Take your time with this energy. When you feel ready to come back, you can slowly take a couple of deep breaths, bring your awareness to your eyes and slowly come back.

◆

Reflections

You have received an initiation and activation as a High Priestess/Priest/Priestex from Mary Magdalene and the Almighty.

The Holy of Holies is a Sacred Chamber whereby the Divine Presence connects directly with you. This is the most powerful energy you could experience as you meet the Divine face to face.

Before getting up, take some time to be in this energy. You have had a very high-frequency initiation and activation. While you are in this energy, spend some time journaling your experience. As you journal, you will still be experiencing the incredible healing power of Mary Magdalene and the Almighty.

After journaling, spend some time letting this energy integrate into your system. You may feel the effects of it for up to 3 weeks. When you have received such high-frequency energy, it is essential to let your physical body slowly adapt to this shift.

Nurture yourself through this transformation by grounding yourself with healthy foods and walks in nature.

Take your time before moving on to the next chapter.

For now, enjoy spending time integrating and writing your experience in your journal.

ALIGNING WITH YOUR DIVINE PURPOSE

CHAPTER 20

BEING GROUNDED

"Connect with Me, and I will guide you to the Great Unknown" - Great Gaia Spirit

I have mentioned the importance of grounding at the end of each initiation and activation. You invite incredibly high-frequency energy into your body during each initiation and activation. Your body may not be used to embodying such high frequencies.

You are now moving towards living a new way of life. This way of life involves continually connecting with the Divine Mind and your Holy Spirit. Through this continual connection, your body will be a fountain of this high-frequency energy. The more you place your awareness toward the Divine Mind and your Holy Spirit, the more you invite this fountain of energy to pour through you continually.

Over time, you may notice your body feeling lighter and lighter. You may feel your body is not experiencing gravity in the same way. This is because your body is becoming a Light Body. Your body is transforming into a Holy Vessel. Your body has been receiving light codes downloaded into your cells, tissues, ligaments, tendons, muscles, blood, and organs.

Your old way of being will not work with this Light Body. Grounding and allowing this energy to flow through you and Mother Earth is essential. It is also necessary to intentionally connect with Mother Earth to experience grounding daily. Your denser body did not require such grounding because it was not receiving such consistent high frequencies travelling through it.

You have invited yourself to connect with your Holy Spirit directly. As a result, you will be experiencing your Holy Spirit embodying your Divine Vessel (your body) at times. As the awareness you place on this connection increases, the more your body will experience a lightness of being. The more you develop this connection, the more it is imperative that you be grounded.

When you are grounded with Mother Earth, you more easily integrate the high-frequency energy your Holy Spirit brings forth.

If you do not practice grounding, you may experience uncomfortable feelings in your body and mind. These feelings could show up in the form of headaches, anxiousness, feeling too high, feeling light-headed, not being able to think straight, not feeling centred, feeling irritated in the body, and having an array of emotions, to name a few.

When living as a Light Being, it is crucial for your body to feel at ease so you can take great joy in Awakening the Goddess Within.

Exercise: Groundedness Awareness

Preparation for Initiation

The first step in understanding the importance of grounding is understanding *how* grounded you genuinely feel.

1. To understand how grounded you feel, write the answers in your journal to the following questions:
    * Do you feel lightheaded when doing energy work or when connecting with the Divine Mind and Holy Spirit?
    * Do you get headaches after connecting?

- Do your emotions go all over the place afterward?
- Do you find your mind gets confused, and you lack a feeling of being centred afterward?
- Does your body start to feel anxious after experiencing a lot of energy work?

◆

Great awareness! Now that you have become more acutely aware of your groundedness, you can place this awareness on yourself daily. You can use this as a compass to reorient yourself to connect with Mother Earth when needed.

◆

Exercise: Grounding

Preparation for Initiation

So, how does one practice grounding? Placing your awareness on Mother Earth is a helpful method for experiencing groundedness. People forget the power Mother Earth has in assisting us with grounding. People also forget the influence that their awareness has. Where your attention goes, energy flows. When you focus on Mother Earth to send you her beautiful energy, you experience her power.

1. Your next exercise is to spend the next week trying different grounding exercises. When you have completed them, come back here and take some notes in your journal as to how they assisted you in feeling grounded. Write down how grounded each particular activity made you feel.

Some methods of getting grounded are:

- Walking in nature. As you walk in nature, focus on the trees, animals, wind, scents, sounds, and soil. As you walk, ask Mother Earth to ground you;
- Lying down on the ground outside. Feel yourself connected to Mother Earth.
- Hugging a tree. You can ask the tree to ground you. Experience the wisdom of the tree. Trees often have excellent guidance to share with you.
- Lying on your bed, closing your eyes and imagining Mother Earth below you. Invite her to send you her grounding energy;
- Eating root vegetables. As you eat these vegetables, ask these vegetables to ground you and connect you to Mother Earth;
- Honouring how food makes you feel and eating those foods that assist you to feel grounded;
- Holding black onyx or other crystals. Ask the crystal to ground you; and
- Exercise. Getting cardio going is a great way to get energy moving through your body so you can feel more grounded.
- Taking a mud bath. Go to a spa and let yourself be treated with a mud bath. Feel the energy of the mud grounding you.

BEING GROUNDED

You have done great work with taking some time to connect with Mother Earth. Keep this pattern going and get yourself to do things throughout each day that assist you in feeling grounded.

Initiation: Connecting with Great Gaia Spirit

Guided by:
Great Gaia Spirit

Close your eyes and take a couple of deep breaths. Feel yourself letting go of what you don't need right now.

Know that whatever your experience is, this is perfect for you and Divinely guided by your Inner Goddess.

Feel the Presence of Great Gaia Spirit come up through the bottoms of your feet.

Feel the pulse of Great Gaia Spirit enter your Base Chakra now.

This pulse moves from your lower body to your upper body until you can feel her pulse throughout your entire body.

As you feel her pulse, breathe in the lovely scent of the organic soil filling the air.

Allow this scent to permeate your nose and fill your body.

"As above, so below," Great Gaia Spirit says.

She smiles at you and welcomes you.

"Welcome home," she says.

"You have made it as an Enlightened Being while stepping on the grounds of Mother Earth.

"It was your destiny to experience this enlightenment while treading across Gaia's soil.

BEING GROUNDED

"Imagine your bare feet walking across my soil now.

"Feel my grounding presence radiate up through your feet and into your entire being.

"Breathe my entire Presence within your body now."

Great Gaia Spirit invites you to take some time to experience her grounded Magnificence to integrate with your entire body, mind, and Soul.

"Remember me when you walk this Earth.

"Be aware that I am with you with each step you take.

"It is through this awareness you can experience my Mightiness.

"It is through this awareness you experience my Great Unknown.

"I am with you always.

"All you need to do is invite me in through your awareness."

Great Gaia Spirit has a gift and initiation to give you that will assist you in aligning with her.

Take some time to receive her gift and initiation now.

Great Gaia Spirit thanks you for connecting so deeply with her.

Take a moment to give thanks to Great Gaia Spirit.

Whenever you are ready, you can slowly take a couple of deep breaths, bring your awareness to your eyes and slowly come back.

Reflections

You have received a sacred initiation from Great Gaia Spirit. She invites you to spend time connecting with her and listening to her Wisdom Stories. She says she has many things to share that have never been heard. "When you connect with me, you will experience the Great Unknown," she says. She refers to "the Great Unknown" as sacred teachings that have been kept in the belly of the Earth. "They are ready to be heard," Beloved Gaia says.

Before getting up, take some time to be in this energy. While you are in this energy, spend some time journaling your experience. As you journal, you will still be experiencing the incredible grounding power of Great Gaia Spirit.

Take your time before moving on to the next chapter.

For now, enjoy spending time integrating and writing your experience in your journal.

BEING GROUNDED

HEAL & AWAKEN THE GODDESS WITHIN

CHAPTER 21

BEING PRESENT

"The Power of Presence Lies in Your Breath" - Buddha

You have now come full circle. You are now at a place where you are ready to be an Enlightened Being and share your unique Divine Gifts in this world. All that is required of you from this point forward is being *present*.

When you live in the present moment, you give yourself the greatest gift of living in your Divine Presence.

With each breath you take, the Divine is breathing your breath. When you place your awareness and attention on who is breathing your breath, you return to the realization of this Magnificence that is living through you.

You now have all the tools to bring forth your greatest gifts and share them with the world. All that is needed is your consistent awareness of your Divine Presence.

When you are present, you remember who you are.

When you live in the present moment, you recall all the tools you can utilize to connect with your Sacred Heart and the Divine Mind, receive the next action steps to take, and move forward with manifesting your Divine Purpose.

There is no more significant time than now to live your Divine Purpose.

Many feel they need to keep learning to be able to move forward. The need to keep learning is a method to keep you feeling safe. It will also keep you from moving forward if all you do is learn and not take action. You have been given the tools to assist you in getting past whatever is holding you back from feeling safe. The next step is permitting yourself to live your Divine Purpose *now*.

The secret sauce to living your Divine Purpose *now* is allowing yourself to live in the present moment. You invite your Divine Presence in when you live in the present moment. Being connected to the Divine Presence is the only way to be present.

So, now, here you are, witnessing the brilliance within you. You have made a connection with your Inner, Sacred Feminine Goddess. You have spoken to her. You have heard her inner desires and seen your incredible strengths. You have mapped out your Divine Purpose. You have uncovered hidden shadows that have held you back from being aware. Now, you stand as your Brilliant Self, shining for the world to see.

You are ready, and all you need to do is permit yourself to be this Brilliant Diamond and allow your Inner Goddess to create, have a voice, sparkle, and radiate out her brilliance. You no longer need to suppress the Sacred Feminine. You can now be in balance with the inner Sacred Masculine and Sacred Feminine at the same time.

At times, it may take great courage to do this. When you feel you need courage, this means fear is coming up. When you return to your breath and the awareness of the Divine Presence, you allow yourself to return to calm and experience the power in the Greatness that flows through you. This power is always with you whenever you need it.

The more you practice present-moment awareness, the more you experience the power of the Divine Holy Presence.

You came here to bring forth your Greatness, and I celebrate your Awakening of the Goddess Within and revealing to the world your incredible Magnificence!

Exercise: Breath Awareness

Preparation for Initiation

This next exercise is so simple, yet it is mighty. You will now take some time to become aware of your Sacred Breath. Your breath, indeed, is very Holy. Your breath is what keeps you alive. It is your breath that you are gifted with every single day. Your breath is the closest connection you have to experience your Divine Presence. Your breath is a gentle reminder of this incredible Presence of yours.

1. Take some time now, for about half an hour and sit comfortably without any distractions, following these steps:

    * Breathe in and out with your belly.
    * Pay attention to the length of your breaths.
    * Allow each breath to get longer to the point that it still feels very comfortable.
    * With each inhalation and exhalation, place your awareness on the fact that the Divine is the One who is inhaling and exhaling each breath you take.
    * Allow yourself to gain greater awareness of the Divine breathing and exhaling each breath of yours.
    * Keep experiencing this until you feel an inner *knowing* inside your body and in your awareness that the Divine is flowing through you and gracefully breathing you.
    * Give thanks for this Sacred Breath.

2. Write in your journal your experience of this connection with the Divine by having gained awareness of the *Source* of your Sacred Breath.

◆

You have done very sacred work just now. I commend you for taking the time to honour your Divine Breath.

◆

Exercise: Breath Awareness During Daily Activities

Preparation for Initiation

Now that you have learned how to become aware of your breath via meditation, you will take this awareness practice to the next level while doing your daily activities.

The more you place this awareness on your breath throughout the day, the more you live in the present moment and experience the Divine Presence flowing through you.

1. Take some time over the next few days and follow these steps throughout each day while you are doing an activity:
   - While doing a busy activity, become aware of your breathing. It could even be while you are working;
   - While doing this activity, breathe in and out with your belly;
   - Pay attention to the length of your breaths;
   - Allow each breath to get longer to the point that it still feels very comfortable;

- With each inhalation and exhalation, place your awareness on the fact that the Divine is breathing each breath;

- Allow yourself to experience the power of the Divine breathing you as you gain greater awareness of this fact;

- Keep experiencing this until you have felt an inner *knowing* inside your body and an awareness that the Divine is flowing through you and gracefully breathing you;

- Give thanks for this Sacred Breath.

2. After a few days of practicing this awareness of your breathing, write in your journal your experience of this connection with the Divine. Have you noticed a greater understanding of Divine Wisdom, Power, and Love flowing through you while you are doing your activities?

◆

Congratulations on taking the time to do this exercise. I know the effort it takes to try this one out. It may not be easy for some, but the rewards are plentiful.

This task is brilliant, as it teaches you how to apply it in your daily life without having to go into meditation and be still. The more you do it, the easier and more natural it will become to do this more consistently. And, the more you do it, the more you experience the Divine Presence flowing through you and giving you Divine Guidance in all aspects of your life.

Initiation: Becoming One with Your Inner Divine Presence

Guided by:
Buddha

Close your eyes and take a couple of deep breaths. Feel yourself letting go of what you don't need right now.

Know that whatever your experience is, this is perfect for you and Divinely guided by your Inner Goddess.

You see before you a large, beautiful Bodhi Tree, and Beloved Buddha is sitting below the tree.

"Come and sit with me, Precious One, by the beloved Bodhi Tree," says Buddha.

"You have been practicing your breath. Come and breathe with me.

"Take a deep breath and feel the stillness at the top and bottom of your breaths.

"When you reach the end of your next inhalation, allow yourself to hold at the top of your breath and feel the stillness in this precious moment.

"When you feel complete in this stillness, release your breath and hold at the end of your exhalation at the bottom of your breath to once again experience this stillness.

BEING PRESENT

"When you feel complete, repeat these cycles of merging with the stillness with each inhalation and exhalation of your breaths.

"Take some time with me now under the tree breathing with me and experiencing Divine Presence within the Power and Stillness of each breath."

Upon your next breath, Buddha takes you down below the Earth, past the tree's roots and into a beautiful Quartz Crystal Cave.

You can smell the water in the air and feel the sacred vibrations from the Crystals surrounding you.

You notice Buddha sitting across from you.

Buddha says to you, "Enjoy this moment and take some time experiencing the wisdom and purity of this crystal cave energy as I initiate you now into the Sanctity of your Inner Divine Presence flowing through you and all around you."

Buddha hands you a crystal as a gift of remembrance.

You experience a sacred energy filling your body as you receive this crystal.

This crystal is yours to reconnect with this sacred cave whenever you wish.

Take some time to experience this precious energy.

You return to the top and find yourself sitting in meditation next to Buddha under the Bodhi tree.

You hear the wind rustling the leaves above you.

You feel the stillness of inner peace fill you even more.

Buddha says to you, "It is here, in this stillness, where you are most at home.

"Breathe this stillness into your breath every day.

"It is here, in this stillness, where you will find me always."

You feel a great love envelop you.

Receive this love from Buddha.

Take a moment to give thanks to Gracious Buddha.

Whenever you are ready, you can slowly take a couple of deep breaths, bring your awareness to your eyes and slowly come back.

Reflections

You have received an initiation from Gracious Buddha to the Sanctity of your Inner Divine Presence.

Buddha invites you to visit this place under the tree every day if you wish.

Before getting up, take some time to be in this energy. While you are in this energy, spend some time journaling your experience. As you journal, you will still be experiencing Buddha's incredible stillness, wisdom, and sacredness.

After journaling, spend some time letting this energy integrate into your system. You may feel the effects of it for up to 3 weeks. When you have received such high-frequency energy, it is essential to let your physical body slowly adapt to this shift.

Nurture yourself through this transformation by grounding yourself with healthy foods and walks in nature.

Take your time before moving on to the next chapter.

For now, enjoy spending time integrating and writing your experience in your journal.

HEAL & AWAKEN THE GODDESS WITHIN

BEING PRESENT

HEAL & AWAKEN THE GODDESS WITHIN

CHAPTER 22

COMING HOME

"You have brought home your Divine Goddess" - Beloved Mary Magdalene

You have arrived. Home, at last. You look around and see your surroundings. It feels familiar, yet different in some way. You wonder why it feels so different. Nothing has been touched in your home, yet you feel like a stranger as you enter each room.

There is a sense of stillness all around. You sit down to take a moment to feel this stillness. As you do, you realize that you are no longer the same person. You have transformed.

"What now?" you think. You begin to realize your old ways of being at your home no longer serve you. You have left those ways of being behind you. You did not bring back the old you to your home. You brought your Holy Spirit home.

You have now fully Awakened the Goddess Within.

During your journey through this book:

* ❖ You have taken steps to address those moments when you feel alone.
* ❖ You released anxiety and cleared ancestral, past-life, and current-life trauma. You have invited your Holy Spirit's greatest desires of expression back into your life. Bravo!

- You have taken steps to honour your Sacred Body and become aware of what foods you invite into your body. You have liberated yourself with the freedom to activate your sexual nature, self-expression, and creativity.

- You now understand the illusion of fear and how to move past this and let these fears go.

- You learned how to connect to and shift your focus on the Divine Mind as you opened your awareness on receiving Divine Guidance that is best for you.

- You have removed stressors from your life and understood the importance of doing this so that you can always be in flow and connected to the Divine.

- You have Awakened to your Divine Passions and Divine Strengths and created your Divine Purpose Map.

- You have boldly embraced your Divine Power and understood the Science of Divine Will and how it works *for* you, knowing you are One with the Divine.

- You learned that to experience Greatness, you must align with it, as Divine Greatness can only be there for you once you *know* this Greatness is *always* present.

- You have called forth the action taker within you by learning to receive Guidance from the Divine Mind on the steps to be taken toward living your Divine Purpose.

- You learned that the Divine Mind is the One who shows you *how* to live your Divine Purpose. You understand that Divine Guidance might not be given in logical, sequential, linear steps from the Limited Mind, as Divine Wisdom operates from the One (Circle) where there is no time and distance.

- You have moved towards aligning with positively driven people who can support you with your profound endeavours toward living your Holy Spirit's calling.
- You have moved past the Corporate Mentality Mindset, so you can move freely on your path and not be limited by performance-based thoughts.
- You have honoured the ancient teachings of money so that you can be in alignment with the Sacred Tides of ebb and flow.
- You have practiced honouring your Magnificence and embracing this Brilliance. You have understood the power of visualization so that the Divine can respond in the likeness and assist with fully manifesting your Divine Purpose.
- You turned towards embracing your own Inner Saviour, shifting your focus to your Inner Power.
- You cleared out your deepest fears hidden in the cellular structure concerning living your Divine Purpose *now* so that you can freely express yourself.
- You practiced aligning with your Divine Purpose and learned the importance of doing this practice every day before you get out of bed and checking in with yourself throughout your day on this alignment. You were shown how to have a mental guidepost that can remind you to be continually oriented toward your Holy Spirit's calling. You have created Vision and Mission Statements that can keep you oriented toward living your Divine Purpose.
- You have taken extra time to get grounded to fully integrate the high-frequency energy channelling through you, resulting from often connecting with the Divine Mind and your Holy Spirit.
- And, finally, you practiced the power of being *present* daily. You were shown how being present in the moment connected you to

the Divine Power, Love, and Wisdom within you. When you are connected to the Divine, you are continually given Guidance on how to stay on track with living your Divine Purpose.

Through this sacred process, you have been gifted with teachings, initiations, and activations from the Great Goddesses and Benevolent Beings. Below are details to remind you of who came through during your sacred initiations and activations, what purpose they served, and what gifts were given to you as a token of remembrance:

- First came Mother Mary to take all your sorrows away. Then came Jesus to share with you his Divine Love. Serapis Bey connected you to the luminescence of your Divine DNA to help your vibration rise to your Divine DNA strands so that you more easily connect to your Holy Spirit.

- Next came Goddesses Sophia and Diana as they assisted you in returning to wholeness. Goddess Sophia cleansed you of current-life trauma and past-life trauma. Goddess Sophia invited you to bring all your desires of expression back into your body. Goddess Diana reminded you of your oneness to the Divine and shared with you how, each month during the full moon, you can give your troubles to her and release what is not whole so that only peace, honour, and love remain.

- Goddess Isis came to unite you with the power of the Inner Sacred Masculine and the beauty of the Inner Sacred Feminine. The lioness energy of the Ascended Lyran Realm came forth to transmute all ancestral trauma. It transformed this into shimmering Golden energy within every cell of your body, invigorating you with the complete balance of your Yin and Yang energy. You were invited to carry the Golden Elixir of Light to remind you of the Sacred Beauty and Incredible Power of the Goddess Lioness within you.

- The Goddess Realm came to fill your body with Goddess Energy and awaken the energy around your pelvis. You received a symbol in your belly to represent your freedom to activate your sexual nature, your freedom of self-expression and your full creativity. Goddess Isis then came with a Sacred Fire to complete the balance between the expression of the creative and sexual Sacred Feminine and the power of the active Sacred Masculine.

- Beloved Quan Yin came and filled your being with compassion and invited you to forgive yourself. She then assisted with the transmutation of all your illusionary thoughts into golden possibilities. Goddess Emmanuella brought back your connection to the Essence of the Divine by activating the Divine Essence of Love, Wisdom, and Power in your Sacred Heart.

- Lord Lanto gifted you with a pendant resting on your Sacred Heart. Goddess Isis then placed a symbol over your third eye to keep you balanced and centred during your connection with the Divine Mind. Lord Lanto placed a mantle of yellowish gold in your Sacred Heart that extended vertically and horizontally from this area. This assisted you in aligning with the Gateway to the Divine Mind, where you can access Divine Wisdom. You were awakened to the Golden Ray of the Divine Mind so that you may live your Divine Purpose.

- Beloved Quan Yin came once more to allow compassionate forgiveness to enter your being. She asked you to invite ease into your life. Archangel Raphael then assisted with releasing burdens from your entire body. He then consecrated you into the Awakening of your Divine Passions. They invited you to return to them whenever you need healing and blessings.

- Beloved Mary Magdalene came to activate your Sacred Heart with the pink flame. This opened the gateway to Divine Love and the embodiment of your Divine Passions. Mary Magdalene invited you to go within your Sacred Heart, where you will find her as the flame of your inspiration.

- Goddess Peddamma showed up to slay all the demons holding you back from living your full potential. All your self-limiting beliefs were being lifted off your Aura and transmuted by Goddess Peddamma, using her golden sword. She placed liquid golden drops from her sword down your crown that spiralled down your spine. She then twined each golden strand from all your past lives into a Divine Golden Rope. The Golden Rope had extended from your spinal column to your Holy Spirit. Beloved Mary Magdalene then came and activated your Passionate Heart. This Passionate Pink Energy expanded from your Sacred Heart and twined with the Golden Rope as it shimmered in gold and pink strands. Your Divine Strengths activated your Divine Passions. Your Holy Spirit climbed down the rope and united with you. A Pink and Golden Pyramid of Protection was placed around you as your sacred vehicle to which you can return daily. This is your Inner Sanctity, where you can go and witness your Divine Purpose unfolding. They invite you to invoke this Sacred Pink and Golden Pyramid around your Aura daily, with the Pink and Golden Rope extending from your spinal column to your Holy Spirit. You may connect with them whenever you wish to help steer you toward the Divine Union with your Strengths and Passions. In this Sacred Pyramid, you can access and explore all your creativities.

- Goddess Athena came to celebrate how far you have come and to show you your Brilliance. Both Goddess Athena and Beloved Mary Magdalene initiated you into communion with your Divine Purpose. They invited you to take Goddess Athena's Strength as a Goddess Warrior and Beloved Mary Magdalene's Passion and make them your own.

COMING HOME

- Your Divine Spirit came down to meet you and Awaken your Divine Heart and Mind with the joyful possibilities that exist within you as you live out your Divine Purpose *now*. You became aligned with Divine Will and witnessed the Divine Will responding to your resonance. You connected to this incredible Power of Divine Will. You connected to the place where all the answers are fully supplied. Divine Power soared through you as you became One with the Divine and your Holy Spirit.

- Eagle Spirit came to unite you with Faith and Divine Knowing. Eagle Spirit initiated you into the reunion with your Divine Eagle Spirit so that you may soar to great heights. It is here where you can experience unique places that cannot be seen with the human eye. Eagle Spirit invited you to fly with him and the Holy Spirit Condors whenever you wish.

- Goddess Daphne assisted you by the beach to have your body become the sail in the wind so that the sail can take you to majestic places. Goddess Sophia then initiated you into your Soul Family once more so you can fully invite them back into your life. Goddess Daphne invites you to connect with her whenever you need guidance from the wind and to experience your most authentic nature. She is often by the beach, immersed in nature. She reminds you that when you connect with nature, you are connecting with your natural self, for you are a part of nature. Goddess Daphne can also assist you in connecting with Beloved Gaia, the Great Spirit of the Earth. Goddess Sophia is here to support you with your creations whenever you need her.

- Elephant Spirit gifted you with a necklace consisting of a colourful array of gemstones to assist you in bringing back all aspects of you into this world. Elephant Spirit initiated you into a return to wholeness. Goddess Athena then came to remind you of your incredible strength and freedom. Goddess Athena invited you to call on her whenever you need assistance to cast away all doubt and feel empowered to be free.

- ❖ Mother Moon Spirit came to be the Light upon your alter. She gifted you with a Divine Coin as a reflection of your worth. She showered coins upon you, with each coin representing the Souls you are about to transform. You then looked down at your luminescent reflection upon the waters as you basked in the Divine Truth of the Sacred Moon within you.

- ❖ Goddess Athena came once more to activate the Magnificence within you. She took you to a place of experiencing the inner knowing of your Brilliance. You witnessed the feeling and visualization of your Beloved Purpose being manifested now.

- ❖ Goddess Quan Yin and Archangel Raphael came to assist you in inviting trust back into your life, and you were bathed with their healing auras. Your Holy Spirit gave you wise teachings regarding Embracing your Internal Saviour and naturally inviting trust back into your life. Goddess Quan Yin and Archangel Raphael gifted you with a token of remembrance you had of the activation of your Sacred Heart to embrace trust. They invited you to call upon them whenever you need a warm embrace.

- ❖ Goddess Hecate came forth to assist you in releasing deep-seated fears that were holding you back from fully living your Divine Purpose. She is here by your side whenever you need her to help you express your intuitive gifts.

- ❖ Lord Lanto and your Holy Spirit came to prepare you before your initiation with Mary Magdalene into the Holy of Holies. Your Holy Spirit gave you Guidance on how to align with your Holy Spirit every day. Mary Magdalene invited you to follow her into a Sacred Chamber and initiated you as a High Priestess/Priest/Priestex into the Holy of Holies. She activated your Sacred Heart, Soul, and mind in alignment with this sacred energy. In this Holy of Holies, you may return to touch hands with the Almighty and be united with the Great Presence I AM THAT I AM. It is here where you are meeting the Divine face to face. You may call upon Beloved Mary Magdalene whenever you wish to activate your connection with the Holy of Holies.

* Beloved Gaia came and sent her energy pulse from your feet up through your base chakra, then through your lower body to your upper body. She invited you to experience her grounding presence radiating up through your feet into your entire Being, including your body, mind, and Soul. She reminded you to connect with her through the awareness of each step you take. She has teachings to share that are from the "Great Unknown," as she describes. She recommends that you listen to her sacred teachings. She gave you a gift and an initiation that will assist you in aligning with her.

* Beloved Buddha invited you to sit with him at the Bodhi tree and practice breathing with him. He asked you to experience the stillness at the bottom and top of each breath. He then took you down to a beautiful Quartz Cave below the tree as he initiated you into the Sanctity of your inner Presence flowing through you and all around you. He gifted you with a crystal to remember this moment and connect you with this sacred cave whenever you wish. Sacred energy filled your body as you held the crystal. You can find Buddha always within the stillness of your breath.

And, here you are—back home as a new person. Your home is not the same. You have changed in ways that cannot be fully described to those who have not experienced this transformation. You have received ancient wisdom teachings that others are not aware of. You have not only come home as a new person—you have made so many new friends from the Benevolent Realm. They are *always* here for you whenever you want to reconnect with them.

Now is the time to *live* this Divine Purpose of yours *fully*. These sacred teachings are always here for you as tools to keep you moving forward. You may have moments when new challenges may arise. You can return to a particular teaching and practice it again during those times of challenge. You will find that new growth opportunities occur each time you go back to do an exercise. Always remember that the Divine is Infinite. This means there are always opportunities for further expansion as we connect to Divine Wisdom, Love, and Power.

There may also be times when you would like to receive an upgrade in your energy and also connect with a Benevolent Being. Follow your heart and go for it when you hear the calling. These initiations and activations are here for you to enjoy and explore. They are Divine Gifts for you to receive whenever your heart so chooses.

◆

Exercise: Reflections on What I Need

Preparation for Sacred Blessing

Take some time to review all you have experienced during your journey here. Recollect all the exercises, initiations and activations you went through in this book. Answer the following questions:

1. What exercises would be helpful for you to go back through now to take yourself to the next level of living your Divine Purpose?

2. What exercises would help you to get past a temporary setback you may be experiencing? Is there something you need healing on?

3. What initiation(s)/activation(s) would be helpful for you to experience right now?

4. Is there any Goddess or Benevolent Being you would like to connect with and get to know more of? If so, what can you do to have this sacred moment? Which initiation/activation would help you to experience this connection?

5. When would you like to take these next steps?

At any time, you can keep coming back to this reflection exercise and check in with yourself. See how you are feeling and ask yourself whether there is any tool you need to go back to in this book to help you to move forward on this beautiful journey of yours.

Remember, you are *not* alone. The Goddesses and other Benevolent Beings are always here to be by your side and assist you on your Divine path. That is what they are here for.

My Divine Purpose here on Mother Earth is to guide you to Heal the Goddess Within *you* so that you may Awaken to your Holy Spirit, hear its Inner Calling and live out your Divine Purpose. I know my Purpose with you has been fulfilled. Thank you for honouring me to be a witness to your Sacred Awakening.

Welcome home!

Sacred Blessing: Coming Home

Guided by:
Beloved Mary Magdalene

Close your eyes and take a couple of deep breaths. Feel yourself letting go of what you don't need right now.

Know that whatever your experience is, this is perfect for you and Divinely guided by your Inner Goddess.

You feel the Divine Presence of Mary Magdalene as she stands before you.

Your Aura immediately fills with her bright yellow and pink Aura.

She walks up to you, takes your hands, and places them on your Sacred Heart.

She smiles at you, holds your hands against your chest and says, "Congratulations, my dear. You have made it home."

You feel so moved by her touch as you feel her hands touching yours.

You finally feel at home with Mary Magdalene standing so close to you.

Mary places her hands on your face and says, "You need not worry anymore, for you have found your Sacred Home.

"This Sacred Home is yours forever."

Mary places a mantle over your shoulders.

COMING HOME

"May this be a remembrance of your Sacred Home.

"It is here where you are always Whole.

"You have mastered your ability to experience Oneness with your Holy Spirit.

"Keep experiencing the joyfulness, love, dedication, and devotion your Holy Spirit has for you so that you may fully live its greatest desires of expression.

"I am here with you always in the Sacred Chamber of your Beloved Heart."

As Mary touches your Sacred Heart, she says, "You may meet me here always.

"I love you.

"Feel my love for you now as I gift you a Sacred Blessing."

Take some time now to experience this Sacred Blessing from Mary Magdalene.

Mary takes you now up to your very own mountaintop.

"See yourself looking down from your mountaintop," Mary says.

As you see yourself looking down from a beautiful mountaintop, you see a whole new vista before you.

This vista looks so different than before.

Everything is even more beautiful than you had ever previously imagined.

"This is your home," Mary says.

"This is your world of immaculate possibilities.

"You have created such a beautiful sight to see.

"I commend you for a job well done.

"You are so blessed.

"Welcome Home, Beloved Goddess."

Take a moment to thank Beloved Mary Magdalene and the Benevolent Realm for being with you and guiding you on your incredible journey back home.

Whenever you are ready, you can slowly take a couple of deep breaths, bring your awareness to your eyes and slowly come back.

Reflections

You have received a final Sacred Blessing from Beloved Mary Magdalene.

Before getting up, take some time to be in this energy. While you are in this energy, spend some time journaling your experience. As you journal, you will still be experiencing the incredible Sacred Blessing from Beloved Mary Magdalene.

After journaling, spend some time letting this energy integrate into your system.

For now, enjoy spending time integrating and reflecting.

COMING HOME

HEAL & AWAKEN THE GODDESS WITHIN

ABOUT THE AUTHOR

Genevieve Taeger
www.liveatransformativelife.com
Instagram: @genevieve.taeger
Facebook: @LiveATransformativeLife

Genevieve Taeger is a Soul Purpose Coach, Channeler, Intuitive Healer, and Reiki Master. She Channels Powerful Healing and Wisdom Teachings from the Goddesses and Benevolent Realm.

At 16, Genevieve first experienced an initiation from approximately 50 blackbirds, taking turns flying within arm's reach along her body from head to toe and calling to her while moving across her as she was lying on a cot in a campsite. That same year, Mother Mary came to her to bless her in her bedroom while she was getting ready for school. Although Genevieve had never experienced anything like this, somehow she knew what was happening, and it felt normal. When Genevieve was 18, she experienced a Sacred Initiation as she united with her Holy Spirit. Genevieve kept all of this a secret.

Up until this point, Genevieve was living a "normal" life. She went to the University of Guelph and earned her B.A. in Music and Geography. She spent the next 30 years working in Environmental, Health and Safety and moved up the ladder into a prominent Leadership Role in the Automotive Sector.

During her 30s, Genevieve secretly received more Guidance, Initiations, and specialized Teachings from various Ascended Masters and other Benevolent Beings. During this time, she longed to quit her job and follow her intuition to live her Purpose, but she was too afraid to take a leap of faith. In her 40s, during her spare time on weekends, she began teaching Reiki and having local Meetup Groups out of her home, sharing teachings from these Benevolent Beings.

While diligently working in the Corporate World, Genevieve kept feeling a strong nudge to live her Purpose and help change a million lives. She kept ignoring this Calling until she had a breakdown when she turned 50. It was then that she decided to have the courage to quit her job, sell her house and take a chance and do what she felt called to do.

She is now taking a stand for others worldwide to Heal the Goddess Within and Awaken to their Purpose so they can share their unique Gifts and live joyous lives. Her goal is to help transform one million lives.

Join Genevieve for a one-of-a-kind opportunity to work directly with her so you can make massive transformations in your life and move towards living your Divine Purpose. You can reach her at www.liveatransformativelife.com.

Printed in Dunstable, United Kingdom